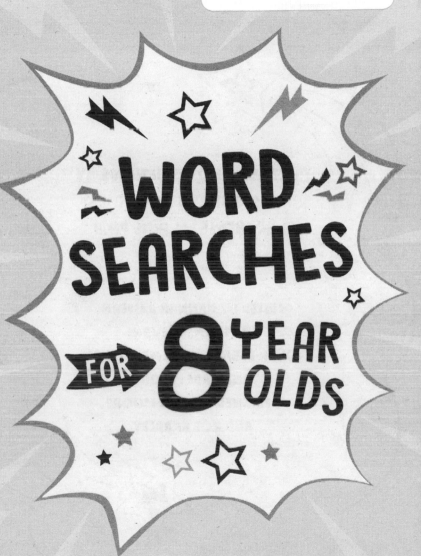

PUZZLES AND SOLUTIONS BY
DR GARETH MOORE
B.SC (HONS) M.PHIL PH.D

EDITED BY HANNAH DAFFERN
AND FRANCES EVANS
COVER DESIGN BY ANGIE ALLISON
AND JADE MOORE
DESIGNED BY JADE MOORE
AND ZOE BRADLEY

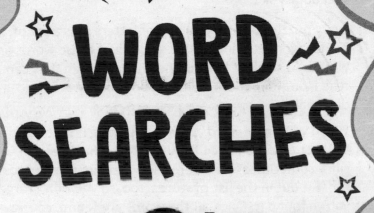

# WORD SEARCHES
## FOR 8 YEAR OLDS

BUSTER BOOKS

# INTRODUCTION

Wordsearches are fun puzzles that anyone can solve. They are a great way to boost your spelling and vocabulary skills.

Every puzzle consists of a grid of letters plus a list of hidden words to find in that grid. All of these words are written in straight lines in the grid, although they can read in any direction, including both backwards and diagonally.

When you find a word, draw a line along it in the grid. It's best to use a pencil for this, or a highlighter pen, since sometimes letters are used again in other words. Cross it out in the list of words, too, so you don't forget you've found it. Once all the words are found, you've finished the puzzle – well done!

Sometimes an entry you're looking for is made up of more than one word, such as 'ICE AGE'. If so, ignore the spaces and search for 'ICEAGE' without a space. If there is punctuation, such as the hyphen in 'T-SHIRT', then ignore that too and search for 'TSHIRT'. It's only ever the letters you are looking for in the grid.

Each puzzle has a different topic, given at the top of the page, but you don't need to know anything about that topic to solve it. In fact, you might learn something new so why not look up any words or names you don't already know?

Some of the grids are in an unusual shape, to match the topic, but this doesn't affect the way you solve the puzzles. Ignore the outlines when solving and pay attention only to the letters.

The puzzles are split into 'Get Started', 'Getting Trickier' and 'Experts Only' sections, and gradually get bigger as you work your way through the book. The solution to every puzzle is given at the back of the book.

Good luck and have fun!

## MISSING MIDDLES

Some of the puzzles have had the middle part of their grids cut out and replaced by dashed-line boxes. So it's up to you to complete the grid! As you work out each letter, write it into the grid. Don't guess, though, because there is only one way to complete the grid while also finding all of the listed words.

Start with a long entry and, if you can't find it in the normal way, try to find its start or end in the grid. Once you locate the start or end, write the missing part of the word into the grid, then cross out the word in the usual way. Keep going, working your way from the longest to the shortest words. If you can't find a word, skip it for now and try another. As you fill in more of the middle, it gets easier.

## INTRODUCING THE WORDSEARCHES MASTER: GARETH MOORE, B.SC (HONS) M.PHIL PH.D

Dr Gareth Moore is an Ace Puzzler and author of many puzzle and brain-training books.

He created an online brain-training site called BrainedUp.com, and runs an online puzzle site called PuzzleMix.com. Gareth has a Ph.D from the University of Cambridge, where he taught machines to understand spoken English.

# 1 SHADES OF PURPLE

```
A M E T H Y S T Y
A I N D I G O R R
T T R D G T R N E
E M N L U E R E D
L U L E B I V S N
O L V L G U M I E
I P U E A A U E V
V M M M B M M D A
C E R I S E N A L
```

AMETHYST
CERISE
INDIGO
LAVENDER
MAGENTA
MAUVE

MULBERRY
PLUM
VIOLET

# COUNTRIES ON THE EQUATOR

2

```
K  L  I  Z  A  R  B  E  S
A  I  B  M  O  L  O  C  E
A  U  R  L  I  N  D  U  V
R  I  G  I  E  M  K  A  I
G  N  L  A  B  E  T  D  D
T  A  N  A  N  A  O  O  L
M  A  B  Y  M  D  T  R  A
A  D  A  O  B  O  A  I  M
I  N  D  O  N  E  S  I  A
```

BRAZIL           MALDIVES
COLOMBIA         SOMALIA
ECUADOR          UGANDA
GABON
INDONESIA
KENYA
KIRIBATI

# THINGS THAT ARE SOFT

```
A E P I L L O W F
N O I H S U C B T
E F E A T H E R E
K B L O Y A A T K
B F W E N E L B N
F E U B E I H N A
L W A R U C E N L
A G L Q K D E N B
T E D D Y B E A R
```

| | |
|---|---|
| BEANBAG | FUR |
| BLANKET | PILLOW |
| CUSHION | QUILT |
| FEATHER | TEDDY BEAR |
| FLEECE | TOWEL |

# CARD GAMES

**4**

```
E B R I D G E R S
C R D W H U U O N
H M I S H M N G E
E E C A M I H O V
A T I Y T W S Y E
T S N A P I B T S
S E D A P S L C M
S W I T C H C O C
C S G O F I S H S
```

BRIDGE        UNO
CHEAT         WHIST
GO FISH
RUMMY
SEVENS
SNAP
SOLITAIRE
SPADES
SWITCH

# 5 SQUARE NUMBERS

```
E S U E I O I D H E
T V Y N E E H E T I
H R I F O U R R D G
I H G F I X E D O H
R H E N Y O U N E T
T Y F N I T S U E Y
Y N E N Y N N H R O
S N N F S F E E E N
I S I X T E E N W E
X N T X E D N O N T
```

**EIGHTY-ONE**
**FOUR**
**NINE**
**ONE HUNDRED**
**SIXTEEN**
**THIRTY-SIX**
**TWENTY-FIVE**

# MUSICAL VOICES

6

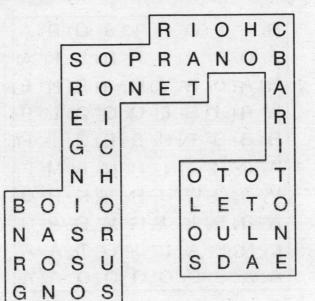

```
            R  I  O  H  C
   S  O  P  R  A  N  O  B
   R  O  N  E  T        A
   E     I              R
   G     C              I
   N     H     O  T  O  T
B  O  I  O     L  E  T  O
N  A  S  R     O  U  L  N
R  O  S  U     S  D  A  E
G  N  O  S
```

ALTO            SINGER
BARITONE        SOLO
BASS            SONG
CHOIR           SOPRANO
CHORUS          TENOR
DUET

# LIQUIDS

**7**

```
R E F C H I S O D A
E O C T I P R L K A
E A O R V U A E K E
A R J E E O G O L E
B E S T C S E G I F
A J R A I R N F M F
V T O W U P I K R O
A S E I J C V E A C
L N E A L J E T A A
A A S D C O O O A A
```

BROTH
COFFEE
JUICE
LAVA
MILK
OIL
SAUCE
SODA
SOUP

TEA
VINEGAR
WATER

# STYLES OF MUSIC

**8**

```
Z D L P A R Z C U S
A A A K N A Z A C K
O N C P C F A K O N
C S I D G O J O A U
S C S F R O R A L F
I I S O I Z S U S I
D N A L J S O P S D
C D L K A S O L E I
P I C O U N T R Y L
R E A R E P O D U L
```

CLASSICAL    ROCK
COUNTRY    SOUL
DISCO
FOLK
FUNK
GOSPEL
INDIE
JAZZ
OPERA
RAP

**9**

# FLUFFY ANIMALS

```
C H I C K S T K E H
H N G H H I L I C E
I O H E B H E T H K
N P E B R Y P T I M
C P A A E B L E P P
H R E M T A I N M U
I I S A S L H L U P
L E U L M A H E N P
L M O L A O P P K Y
A G M M H K E E I M
```

CHICK
CHINCHILLA
CHIPMUNK
GERBIL
HAMSTER
KITTEN
KOALA
LLAMA

MOUSE
PUPPY
RABBIT
SHEEP

# TEAM SPORTS

**10**

```
B E G N I L C Y C V
A S L L A B T F O S
S S E A O G O L C A
K O R Y S R L L F I
E R B A S E B A L L
T C O F Y L R B A I
B A H B Y A T T O N
A L A O V Y V O A G
L L K G N I W O R G
L H O C K E Y F A A
```

| | |
|---|---|
| BASEBALL | ROWING |
| BASKETBALL | SAILING |
| CYCLING | SOFTBALL |
| FOOTBALL | VOLLEYBALL |
| HOCKEY | |
| LACROSSE | |
| LASER TAG | |
| RELAY | |

# TYPES OF BAG

```
D U F F E L S K S S
T B A H O R C U E H
S O R O O A I S H O
N S H T S T A C H U
U C C K C C T A K L
S O C A F U N F D D
D U S E L D D A S E
R E I C B T O T E R
C R B A C K P A C K
B I G N I P P O H S
```

BACKPACK
BRIEFCASE
CLUTCH
DOCTOR'S
DUFFEL
HANDBAG
RUCKSACK

SADDLE
SCHOOL
SHOPPING
SHOULDER
SUITCASE
TOTE

# COASTAL FEATURES 12

```
H C P I N L E T I S
E F L U G P P G T G
A T Y E A L E I Y I
D E H C A L N C R D
L L D A C R I L A N
A S C O Y B N I U A
N I V A E C S F T L
D E D A V A U F S S
P I C U I E L A E I
U H A B A Y A L T D
```

| | |
|---|---|
| BAY | INLET |
| BEACH | ISLAND |
| CAPE | ISLET |
| CAVE | PENINSULA |
| CLIFF | |
| COVE | |
| ESTUARY | |
| GULF | |
| HEADLAND | |

# 13 WINDY WORDS

```
W O Y R R U L F U E
H G T N E R R U C R
I L B R E E Z E R R
R W F L R H T B H C
L O L S G W R S Y B
F H P U F F O C U R
H T A E R B L L N G
Y E L A G O L Y B W
T F A W N R W U U W
N E W E W H O O S H
```

BLOW
BREATH
BREEZE
CURRENT
CYCLONE
FLURRY
GALE
GUST
HOWL
PUFF

WAFT
WHIRL
WHOOSH

# FIND A ROUTE

```
O  A  V  E  N  U  E  L  S  V
O  E  K  P  A  T  H  S  T  L
W  G  C  W  H  A  A  E  R  K
T  R  A  I  L  P  E  Y  P  W
S  L  R  C  R  R  E  A  O  A
A  L  T  E  T  L  S  W  S  L
L  E  D  S  L  S  W  H  S  K
W  N  W  A  A  L  G  A  W
U  A  Y  G  R  W  E  I  A  A
K  L  E  R  O  A  D  H  G  Y
```

| | |
|---|---|
| ALLEY | STREET |
| AVENUE | TRACK |
| HIGHWAY | TRAIL |
| LANE | UNDERPASS |
| PASSAGE | WALKWAY |
| PATH | |
| ROAD | |

# 15 COLD COUNTRIES

```
I A I L O G N O M D
C A E N A E Z R A N
E D I S O T T I W A
L A L S T R V C A L
A N D I S O W I K N
N A O K O U N A A I
D C H I N A R I Y F
K A Z A K H S T A N
S W E D E N M A R K
N A T S Z Y G R Y K
```

| | |
|---|---|
| CANADA | KYRGYZSTAN |
| CHINA | LATVIA |
| DENMARK | MONGOLIA |
| ESTONIA | NORWAY |
| FINLAND | RUSSIA |
| ICELAND | SWEDEN |
| KAZAKHSTAN | |

# IT'S A LIST

16

```
Y  T  S  I  L  K  C  E  H  C
Y  R  O  T  N  E  V  N  I  O
S  R  A  R  E  T  S  O  R  N
Y  A  E  L  A  R  O  T  A  T
L  D  X  G  U  G  R  E  U  E
L  N  Y  E  I  B  E  C  D  N
A  E  A  B  D  S  A  N  E  T
B  L  E  B  S  N  T  C  D  S
U  A  S  M  E  T  I  E  O  A
S  C  H  E  D  U  L  E  R  V
```

AGENDA
CALENDAR
CHECKLIST
CONTENTS
INDEX
INVENTORY
ITEMS
REGISTER
ROSTER
ROTA

SCHEDULE
SYLLABUS
VOCABULARY

# 17 BURGER TOPPINGS

```
M O O R H S U M O L
E A O D A C O V A N A C
O S O E P U H C T E K C
  I H F E N E O P
  B L A I R N U A A U
  H A E N T I N A L G
  S C T N O E H A
  S T I O T O M D J A
  M O L N U Y A E
  A E S E E H C A T G
S M U S T A R D E M O G
R O N O I N O D E I R F
```

AVOCADO
BACON
CHEESE
FRIED EGG
FRIED ONION
JALAPENO
KETCHUP
LETTUCE
MAYONNAISE
MUSHROOM
MUSTARD

RELISH
TOMATO

# ROCK-POOLING

```
S N M D E E W A E S
P T I S E L I A N S
O M U H I U E B T P
N L U M C N R A C M
G E P S O R R R R I
E E L M S F U N A R
T E E K I E R A B H
K N K S N C L C E S
A E H E B I K L S S
S W H E L K W E N H
```

| | |
|---|---|
| ANEMONE | SEAWEED |
| BARNACLE | SHRIMP |
| CRAB | SNAIL |
| KELP | SPONGE |
| LIMPET | STARFISH |
| MUSSEL | WHELK |
| SEA URCHIN | WINKLE |

# 19 SPORTS EQUIPMENT

```
R T A B N D S T S N
A L A B U L C E E E
C L K L G S T S M T
K A E L E A H P R S
E B L V K E L U S K
T A O S L A N T M I
N L T M O K P L E S
G K E G S E N R T A
T T T S P A R T S E
L S D A P U O T E S
```

| | |
|---|---|
| BALL | PADS |
| BAT | RACKET |
| CLUB | SKATES |
| GLOVES | SKIS |
| GOAL | STRAPS |
| HELMET | TRUNKS |
| NET | |

# RIVERSIDE WALK 20

```
S T O P H S R C L S
N R S G S T N L D H
A E K E I A A U L T
W E C E F F C O S A
S S U S R K A E B P
H I D E L T N U D T
K P T I O T T E R O
E A N E G D I R B O
W G J E T T Y U R F
S S D E E R T T D E
```

BOAT
BRIDGE
DUCKLINGS
DUCKS
FISH
FOOTPATH
GEESE
JETTY
NEST
OTTER
REEDS
SWANS

TREES
WATERFALL

# 21 STORY GENRES

```
H R O M A N C E E E
D I Y D O R A P R S
E R S C I F I O U Y
T O E T M O L P T S
E R Y L O K E R N A
C R P Y L R M F E T
T O S O H I I A V N
I H F E F A R C D A
V H R Y M E C H A F
E O C O M E D Y T L
```

ADVENTURE
COMEDY
CRIME
DETECTIVE
FANTASY
FOLKLORE
HISTORICAL
HORROR
PARODY
ROMANCE

SCI-FI
SPY
SUPERHERO
THRILLER

# ALL ABOUT BIRDS

22

| D | D | O | O | R | B | H | R | C | R |
|---|---|---|---|---|---|---|---|---|---|
| E | N | I | D | C | C | E | R | Y | E |
| G | E | G | N | T | H | O | A | T | H |
| D | S | T | A | T | O | L | A | T | C |
| E | T | H | A | S | P | R | F | E | L |
| L | Y | E | T | S | G | F | G | C | W |
| F | F | K | I | I | E | R | H | I | N |
| I | L | D | M | E | E | I | N | N | G |
| H | Y | E | D | A | C | G | L | D | G |
| F | F | S | R | K | C | A | A | A | E |

| | |
|---|---|
| BROOD | FLY |
| CHICK | HATCH |
| DISPLAY | MIGRATE |
| EGG | NEST |
| FEATHER | REAR |
| FEED | ROOST |
| FLEDGE | WING |

# 23 SHIMMER AND SHINE

```
G T W I N K L E F I
S L E L K R A P S C
C H H R E M M I L G
G L I T T E R R A G
D E L M R F E P L L
A R N I M K L I A I
Z A W I C E S A F N
Z L O I H T R L S T
L G L P E S T E E H
E F G N K M A E L G
```

**DAZZLE**          **SPARKLE**
**FLASH**           **TWINKLE**
**FLICKER**
**GLARE**
**GLEAM**
**GLIMMER**
**GLINT**
**GLISTEN**
**GLITTER**
**GLOW**
**SHIMMER**
**SHINE**

# IN THE HOME 24

```
O  B  R  G  L  E  L  B  A  T
S  O  O  D  U  B  B  O  A  L
P  O  R  E  A  R  D  R  O  C
M  K  R  S  A  R  C  O  U  B
A  C  I  K  E  A  T  P  E  R
L  A  M  S  R  S  B  A  P  R
F  S  S  P  S  O  N  B  A  I
K  E  E  O  A  B  E  K  M  A
R  T  F  R  A  D  O  T  S  H
S  A  D  G  O  K  C  O  L  C
```

| | |
|---|---|
| BEANBAG | DRESSER |
| BED | LAMP |
| BOOKCASE | MIRROR |
| CARPET | RUG |
| CHAIR | SOFA |
| CLOCK | STOOL |
| CUPBOARD | TABLE |
| DESK | |

# TYPES OF PEN

25

```
F R R N L U N H T R R
I N T T R I R R O N E
S K M L I E E L I I N
I R N S F K L A T T I
L O N T R E T L F L L
T F O A R N L L R O E
L I M B U T E T A A N
E L A O S U L Y T S I
G L F E I L T O L I F
L T N I O P L L A B P
H I G H L I G H T E R
```

**BALLPOINT**
**FELT-TIP**
**FINELINER**
**FOUNTAIN**
**GEL**
**HIGHLIGHTER**
**MARKER**

**ROLLERBALL**
**STYLUS**

# 26 SCIENCE LAB

| | | | | | | | | |
|---|---|---|---|---|---|---|---|---|
| F | N | R | E | R | R | I | T | S | C | M |
| I | S | M | R | R | R | L | H | R | I | L |
| L | P | R | E | C | R | E | E | C | P | E |
| T | A | A | K | M | S | E | R | P | E | N |
| E | T | D | A | D | L | O | M | C | T | N |
| R | U | R | E | D | S | K | O | L | R | U |
| P | L | O | B | C | N | S | M | A | I | F |
| A | A | P | O | R | C | A | E | M | D | D |
| P | C | P | D | O | R | L | T | P | I | H |
| E | E | I | P | F | F | E | S | S | M |
| R | T | R | C | S | S | R | R | R | H | I |

BEAKER
CLAMP
DROPPER
FILTER PAPER
FLASK
FUNNEL
MICROSCOPE
PETRI DISH
SPATULA
STAND

STIRRER
THERMOMETER

# PARTS OF A TRAIN 27

```
L G O E B S W N G N N
U U S K P V E S O A O
H W G E N G I N E O I
V B S G K T A I G E S
E A E E A N A G C E N
N C E H S G B E C K E
T S E D L L E G S A P
S T H G I L E R N R S
B E I S A A G E A B U
A W O D N I W E H C S
W I I N A K S G T W K
```

BRAKE            SUSPENSION
CAB              VENTS
ENGINE           WHEEL
LIGHTS           WINDOW
LUGGAGE RACK
SEAT

# 28 TYPES OF PASTA

```
L I N G U I N E I I E
I E N T O T N N L L I
T L R I L I L N L O N
T L I F L Z Z E E I O
E A I U P L T P C V T
H F T S P A E I I A A
G R T I I I L T M R G
A A N L C E L N R O I
P F G L T G V M E O R
S A R I E N N I V S T
T I N O L L E N N A C
```

CANNELLONI    TORTELLINI
FARFALLE    VERMICELLI
FUSILLI    ZITI
LINGUINE
PENNE
RAVIOLI
RIGATONI
SPAGHETTI
TAGLIATELLE

# IT'S A DREAM

**29**

```
G E N F L M N X G I Y
C X O A A T R O T N E
M P I N E A A O O O A
A E T T D L I I W I R
E C A A I P T I E T N
R T N S N I S I P A I
D A I Y B H N G O R N
Y T G M P P N T H I G
A I A E R I S E D P I
D O M V I S I O N S D
R N I T L A T N G A R
```

AMBITION

ASPIRATION

DAYDREAM

DESIRE

EXPECTATION

FANTASY

GOAL

HOPE

IDEAL

IMAGINATION

VISION

WISH

YEARNING

# MAKING ENERGY

**MISSING MIDDLE** For instructions on how to do this puzzle, turn back to the introduction.

```
E E N A P O R P Y T C
I B I O M A S S T D O
N T U R B I N E I I A
O A W A V E S H C E L
I G W I       E I S R
S C E M       N R E A
S I S I       L T L E
I O O O H I L R C S L
F N G T S S A G E T C
R E E U I H O G L I U
N M F R A L O S E M N
```

BIOMASS
COAL
DIESEL
ELECTRICITY
FISSION
FUSION
GAS
HYDROGEN
METHANE
NUCLEAR

OIL
PROPANE
SOLAR
TURBINE
WAVES
WIND

# DRAWING TIME

**31**

```
W K E L B B I R C S P
N E S E T D P E O O D
S S T J L O E O D E S
H L O T R D U P S E S
A T W T E T O I I U K
D R R A L U G O T C E
E A I I R N O Y D D T
Y C N W T C I H P N C
U E K R A M S M L O H
R P I C T U R E S I C
I L L U S T R A T E S
```

COPY
DEPICT
DESIGN
DOODLE
ILLUSTRATE
JOT
MARK
OUTLINE
PICTURE
PORTRAY

SCRAWL
SCRIBBLE
SHADE
SILHOUETTE
SKETCH
TRACE

# 32 IT CONTAINS "TEN"

```
A  N  E  T        A  T  T  E  N  D  C
N  A  T  E        S  T  A  N  N  O  S
T  E  T  N        I  N  T  E  N  N  S
E  F  S  L        N  I  T  T  A  S  E
N  A  E  A        X  E        N  O  N
I  S  P  I        E  N  N     T  F  T
N  T  R  T        T  I  T     E  T  E
T  E  E  N        T  N  I     N  E  N
E  N  T  E        O  C  O  D  N  N  C
N  C  E  T        R  O  N  N  A  C  E
S  I  N  O        U  T  E  N  S  I  L
E  L  D  P        N  E  T  S  I  L  N
```

| | |
|---|---|
| ANTENNA | POTENTIAL |
| ATTEND | PRETEND |
| ATTENTION | ROTTEN |
| CONTENT | SENTENCE |
| EXTEND | SOFTEN |
| FASTEN | STENCIL |
| INTENSE | TENNIS |
| LISTEN | UTENSIL |

# THINGS THAT ARE SLIPPERY

**33**

```
L  S  L  M  E  C  I  L  S  W  S
P  O  L  I  S  H  E  E  O  L  L
L  M  U  D  W  H  L  N  I  E  F
A  M  E  A  S  D  S  M  E  S  E
L  E  I  U  D  E  E  P  R  E  X
H  C  L  U  M  F  A  E  L  H  A
G  S  P  L  S  N  B  S  L  S  W
L  L  N  W  A  P  S  G  O  R  F
L  A  I  N  S  I  E  F  I  S  H
U  E  A  O  E  S  O  A  P  A  C
D  B  G  R  E  A  S  E  P  A  I
```

| | |
|---|---|
| BANANA PEEL | OIL |
| EELS | POLISH |
| FISH | PUDDLES |
| FROGSPAWN | SLIME |
| GREASE | SLUSH |
| ICE | SNOW |
| LEAF MULCH | SOAP |
| MUD | WAX |

# 34 THINGS THAT ARE HARD

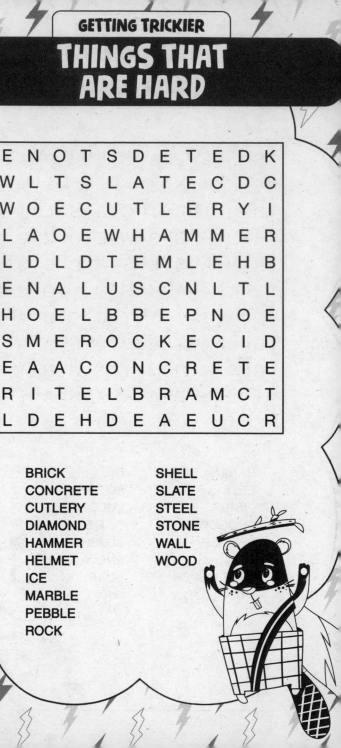

```
E N O T S D E T E D K
W L T S L A T E C D C
W O E C U T L E R Y I
L A O E W H A M M E R
L D L D T E M L E H B
E N A L U S C N L T L
H O E L B B E P N O E
S M E R O C K E C I D
E A A C O N C R E T E
R I T E L B R A M C T
L D E H D E A E U C R
```

BRICK
CONCRETE
CUTLERY
DIAMOND
HAMMER
HELMET
ICE
MARBLE
PEBBLE
ROCK

SHELL
SLATE
STEEL
STONE
WALL
WOOD

# SCHOOL UNIFORM 35

```
R B B L A Z E R A I Z
E L R S S L T A E H R
S H I R T C S S E T O
E N H B S W E O Z B T
R R A S E S R C C S K
S I A A K R C I G S K
O S T C T T B S B A T
B E O T E R E E A R I
R S M R M I G O R T E
I Z K E A K A H A T A
S A T G N S B S S K E
```

| | |
|---|---|
| BAG | SKIRT |
| BLAZER | SOCKS |
| CREST | SWEATER |
| NAME | TIE |
| SHIRT | |
| SHOES | |

# 36 AT THE DENTIST

```
F  T  M  E  D  E  N  T  I  S  T
E  L  O  R  A  T  E  E  T  H  E
G  T  O  O  T  H  P  A  S  T  E
G  E  L  S  T  I  S  U  U  U  S
N  N  H  I  S  H  R  M  Q  H  M
I  A  S  O  E  B  P  A  U  L  I
L  M  I  N  H  T  L  I  C  G  L
L  E  L  T  A  P  A  I  C  D  E
I  L  O  B  R  A  C  E  S  K  R
F  O  P  E  D  I  R  O  U  L  F
T  D  M  O  U  T  H  W  A  S  H
```

| | |
|---|---|
| BRACES | MOUTHWASH |
| DENTIST | PLAQUE |
| ENAMEL | POLISH |
| EROSION | SMILE |
| FILLING | TEETH |
| FLOSS | TOOTHBRUSH |
| FLUORIDE | TOOTHPASTE |
| GUMS | TOOTHPICK |

# GOING TO THE AIRPORT

**37**

```
O G D C U S T O M S I
K S E E Y T I C K E T
T T P E G N U O L A S
X R A Y M A C H I N E
E O R P F R G U N T C
U P T L A U C G A T U
E S U A Y A A X U V R
U S R N F T I T U L I
Q A E E E S P O H S T
R P S C H E C K I N Y
T T S A R R I V A L S
```

ARRIVALS
CAFES
CHECK-IN
CUSTOMS
DEPARTURES
GATE
LOUNGE
LUGGAGE
PASSPORTS
PLANE

QUEUE
RESTAURANTS
SECURITY
SHOPS
TAXIS
TICKET
X-RAY MACHINE

# 38 GARDEN JOBS

**MISSING MIDDLE**

For instructions on how to do this puzzle, turn back to the introduction.

```
E P W E P Y E C T G E
E I P O P P R O P N E
R W E L S Y G M E L Z
P E A K P I H P E M I
N N T R       O W O L
T R U A       S S W I
R N I U       T L P T
E I M L A P W T L I R
G E O H M R E R R Y E
I E S H E A R E R I F
D A T W E Y K C I P M
```

COMPOST
DIG
FERTILIZE
HOE
MOW
MULCH
PICK
PLANT
PRUNE

RAKE
SHEAR
SOW
SPRAY
SWEEP
TRIM
WATER
WEED

# BOWLING ALLEY 39

```
E K F B S T R I K E C
R H O A E V R U C L O
O H U C F R F P M U B
C N L K I K T E A M P
S S B S A P U B K A S
P P Y W O A O G C T H
S L E I G W U I A F O
P I L N L T D B R S E
A T L G T N U A L W S
R S A E A E M S N I P
E U R H P E N A L B S
```

ALLEY
BACKSWING
BOWL
BUMPER
CURVE
FOUL
FRAME
GUTTER
HANDICAP
LANE

PINS
SCORE
SHOES
SPARE
SPLIT
STRIKE
TEAM

# THINGS YOU CAN SEND

**40**

| | | | | | | | | | |
|---|---|---|---|---|---|---|---|---|---|
| P | X | P | R | R | E | T | T | E | L | I |
| I | P | W | O | E | T | F | I | G | F | L |
| N | E | H | E | S | P | M | T | B | R | E |
| O | S | A | C | N | T | O | L | O | E | G |
| T | R | T | L | E | V | C | R | X | P | A |
| E | E | S | L | G | P | E | A | T | L | S |
| E | W | A | I | A | A | T | L | R | Y | S |
| T | O | P | A | K | R | O | T | O | D | E |
| E | L | P | M | C | C | M | T | E | P | M |
| X | F | A | E | A | E | E | A | K | D | E |
| T | F | L | T | P | L | M | S | S | L | A |

BOX
EMAIL
ENVELOPE
FLOWERS
GIFT
LETTER
MEMO
MESSAGE
NOTE
PACKAGE

PARCEL
POSTCARD
REPLY
REPORT
TEXT
WHATSAPP

# THINGS YOU CAN PICKLE

```
R N I K R E H G A S R
T U N L A W O N U E C
H E R R I N G G W U G
R E G N I G A O C R N
R G B O O R L U E O R
E I N K A F M E M E T
P I R P I B N E P E O
P A S L E B L G E N R
E A U R E H S I D A R
P A J A L A P E N O A
C W N E G A B B A C C
```

ASPARAGUS

CABBAGE

CARROT

CAULIFLOWER

CUCUMBER

EGG

GHERKIN

GINGER

GREEN BEAN

HERRING

JALAPENO

LEMON

OKRA

ONION

PEPPER

RADISH

WALNUT

# 42 OBSTACLE COURSE

```
R A B E L L I H L C O
L L B C L R C W L C R
N A H M R T A A U O J
B D H H I R E L P N K
P D I D C L D E X E C
H E A O B R C E R H O
O R R C N T U N N E L
R E C N A L A B C R B
D T H R M P N C J T B
I P J U M P C M H B O
T E N U R H O O P N X
```

| | |
|---|---|
| ARCH | HOOP |
| BALANCE | JUMP |
| BAR | LADDER |
| BLOCK | NET |
| BOX | ROPE |
| CLIMB | RUN |
| CONE | TUNNEL |
| CRAWL | |
| DITCH | |
| HILL | |

# YOUR DIGESTIVE SYSTEM

**43**

```
T W S T O M A C H A D
B B A D U I T U B N E
H A R T E E B S U V W
T C O E E E O T L E D
U T T T V R R O H O T
O E H T B I S C O R A
M R O V E S L F L I E
A I E N I T S E T N I
C A T D Y E N D I K S
I S W A L L O W H T N
D V M T O N G U E U T
```

ABSORB
ACID
BACTERIA
CHEW
DISSOLVE
EAT
FOOD
INTESTINE
KIDNEY
LIVER
MOUTH

NUTRIENT
STOMACH
SWALLOW
TEETH
TONGUE
WATER

# FACE PAINTING

```
S C G R E T A W U D E
N P H L S L I O N E A
E W O H O T B R U S H
G H D N C W E F O I J
L I E A G T P N L G E
I S E A E E A A C N W
T K D A L H S P I I E
T E A R L O E T E N L
E R H T E C I R O Y T
R S S K E E H C O P E
Y L F R E T T U B F S
```

| | |
|---|---|
| ART | JEWEL |
| BRUSH | LION |
| BUTTERFLY | SHADE |
| CHEEK | SPONGE |
| DESIGN | SPOTS |
| EYEPATCH | STENCIL |
| FOREHEAD | WATER |
| GLITTER | WHISKERS |
| GLOW PAINT | |

# A TYPICAL DAY

**45**

```
P R D R E A M K N U R
K E K R O W A U T O L
E L E K O N W R I T E
S M A L D N A T S K A
E N O W S N A R M K D
A S G H E R E P A A T
T S P T E A S G I P E
N A S E D M O L A L G
C I L S A O O K R A M
L K E K U K O C E Y P
W C D T E T K N I R D
```

COME HOME
DREAM
DRINK
EAT
GO OUT
LISTEN
PLAY
READ
RUN

SIT
SLEEP
SPEAK
STAND
TALK
WALK
WORK
WRITE

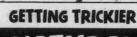

# NATURAL LANDSCAPE FEATURES

**46**

**MISSING MIDDLE**

For instructions on how to do this puzzle, turn back to the introduction.

```
W S L L A F R E T A W
T O W G N T R E S E D
S O V A L A K E S N E
E D C M M A G A I O O
R A T E ☐ ☐ ☐ A G J N
O V E V ☐ ☐ ☐ I U W C
F G R S ☐ ☐ ☐ N E R L
W O N E U L G C E R E
O R C O V L L E L E V
O G M R E I K E T O L
D E H I L L R A Y E V
```

| | |
|---|---|
| CREEK | RIVER |
| DESERT | SEA |
| FOREST | SWAMP |
| GLACIER | VALLEY |
| GORGE | VOLCANO |
| HILL | WATERFALL |
| JUNGLE | WOOD |
| LAKE | |
| MOUNTAIN | |
| OCEAN | |

# AT SCHOOL 47

```
T E A C H E R S C D C
S K S E D C L A N O O
P G O G H I F U S L M
O C Y A C E O S I O P
R M I N T R T B O S U
T R E E G E R R S N T
S P R Y L A S E K O E
S I A I R S N U O S R
A L O Y A E E G O S S
P T E L N K P C B E O
S T C E J B U S R L A
```

BOOKS
CAFETERIA
CHAIRS
CLASSROOM
COMPUTERS
DESKS
GYM
LESSONS
LIBRARY
PENCILS

PENS
PLAYGROUND
SPORTS
SUBJECTS
TEACHERS
TOILETS

# THINGS THAT ARE ROUND

**48**

```
G P O Y O Y H M N B P
L A L I B A A T O I O
O N E L L R O T L A O
B C L O B R T R A E H
E A T L T L A Z Z I P
B K E I E E L E E H W
C E L T P L E G A B E
N L O R I N G N I O C
A P L T E L E C A R B
E C A F K C O L C T N
L H R T H E S U N I T
```

| | |
|---|---|
| BAGEL | MARBLE |
| BALL | PANCAKE |
| BOTTLE TOP | PEARL |
| BRACELET | PIZZA |
| CLOCK FACE | RING |
| COIN | THE SUN |
| GLOBE | TORTILLA |
| HALO | WHEEL |
| HOOP | YO-YO |

# LET'S DANCE

49

| V | I | S | P | I | N | L | S | K | I | P |
|---|---|---|---|---|---|---|---|---|---|---|
| P | P | O | B | E | T | P | I | A | H | I |
| S | E | K | A | H | S | J | Y | P | T | D |
| R | P | A | T | S | A | S | W | A | Y | G |
| P | T | F | L | P | P | E | A | E | C | R |
| H | I | I | I | E | L | E | L | L | L | O |
| L | D | S | L | I | K | T | T | T | A | O |
| E | E | V | R | G | T | W | S | S | P | V |
| U | V | I | I | O | L | U | I | I | U | E |
| D | I | L | W | O | I | I | R | O | W | E |
| E | J | B | T | B | O | I | G | N | U | T |

BOOGIE
BOP
CLAP
DIP
GROOVE
JIVE
LEAP
LIFT
SHAKE
SKIP
SLIDE

SPIN
STEP
SWAY
TAP
TURN
TWIRL
TWIST

# 50 ROAD TRIP

```
D K C S P G N S M O T
G I C I S C O E U U L
D I R A F A I M S H E
E S B E N F T A I I B
L P R R C S A G C G T
A Y E E E T G R T H A
Y R A V T D I E T W E
U A K I U A V O L A S
D D S R O O A C N Y M
T I N D R R N L A S A
N O T R A V E L G R P
```

| | |
|---|---|
| BREAKS | MUSIC |
| CAR | NAVIGATION |
| DELAY | RADIO |
| DIRECTIONS | ROAD |
| DRIVER | ROUTE |
| GAMES | SEATBELT |
| GPS | SNACK |
| HIGHWAY | TRAFFIC |
| I SPY | TRAVEL |
| MAP | |

# FEELING UNSTEADY

```
E K A U Q S H A K E Y
R D R T L L A F S R A
E O E D R E T T L T W
B T T O N E A D Y O S
Q E T D E G M B L P W
U E O D G L E B N P A
I T T E E L B A L L D
V E R R B E E M T E D
E R R B U L V U U P L
R Y O H C R U L M T E
A W F R E V A W H E S
```

DODDER
FALL
LEAN
LURCH
QUAKE
QUIVER
SHAKE
STAGGER
STUMBLE
SWAY
TEETER

TOPPLE
TOTTER
TREMBLE
WADDLE
WAVER
WOBBLE

# 52 TRIP TO THE MOVIES

**MISSING MIDDLE** For instructions on how to do this puzzle, turn back to the introduction.

```
M S C N R O C P O P I
D O S R S S K C A N S
T N V D E E M J Y A U
I N U I A D A A R C B
C E S O       T O T T
K E O I       T T O I
E R U R       N S R T
T C N E C E U M E S L
R S D R I N K S E S E
P R O J E C T O R H S
E T R A I L E R H B T
```

ACTORS
ADS
AISLE
CREDITS
DARKNESS
DRINKS
MOVIE
POPCORN
PROJECTOR
SCREEN

SEAT
SNACKS
SOUND
STORY
SUBTITLES
SURROUND
THEMES
TICKET
TRAILER

# GETTING A HAIRCUT

**53**

```
C L I P L S P R A Y C
S R O S S I C S M O N
R L R U C I L I N O O
C O M B I L R D R O L
R E Y R D R I A H P A
C U T A O T K D E M S
G H R R I A Y N O A W
E I A O E E N I H A
L L N I B R U S H S S
I E R E R L E W O T H
R E S S E R D R I A H
```

BRUSH
CHAIR
CLIP
COMB
CONDITIONER
CURL
CUT
DYE
GEL
HAIRDRESSER
HAIRDRYER

MIRROR
SALON
SCISSORS
SHAMPOO
SINK
SPRAY
TOWEL
WASH

# 54 AT THE ICE RINK

```
N I P S E C A L D E I
E D E E P S L E D C L
L A D E C A C I E N E
Y T L D F N L H P S L
T U O I A S O A D K E
S R C L A C R A J A A
E N A G K T N Y U T P
E B A E N C R A M E N
R D Y E E S L I P S F
F E R F O O T W O R K
K N E D A L B T F I L
```

BALANCE
BLADE
COLD
DANCE
FALL
FOOTWORK
FREESTYLE
GLIDE
ICE HOCKEY
JUMP

LACES
LEAP
LIFT
PARTNER
SKATES
SLIDE
SLIP
SPEED
SPIN
TURN

# MAKING A SCRAPBOOK

```
S  N  I  K  P  A  N  D  M  S  D
O  T  K  P  L  M  R  N  A  T  C
P  D  E  L  O  A  L  O  P  I  O
M  T  I  L  W  S  R  T  R  C  U
A  S  A  I  F  E  T  E  T  K  P
T  A  N  P  T  A  U  C  T  E  O
S  G  W  T  E  L  E  L  A  R  N
E  T  E  K  C  I  T  L  G  R  O
T  L  R  E  C  E  I  P  T  T  D
E  T  A  C  I  F  I  T  R  E  C
P  H  O  T  O  A  A  W  A  R  D
```

| | |
|---|---|
| AWARD | NOTE |
| CERTIFICATE | PHOTO |
| COUPON | POSTCARD |
| DRAWING | RECEIPT |
| GLUE | STAMP |
| LEAFLET | STICKER |
| LETTER | TAG |
| LIST | TAPE |
| MAP | TICKET |
| NAPKIN | |

# 56

# IT'S HOT

| O | T | E | R | E | A | O | C | O | C | P |
|---|---|---|---|---|---|---|---|---|---|---|
| S | R | U | E | V | R | T | P | I | S | U |
| E | N | C | M | O | R | A | A | T | R | O |
| G | U | E | A | T | N | M | E | A | C | S |
| B | S | B | L | S | G | A | D | B | K | T |
| O | E | R | F | A | M | I | L | E | E | A |
| N | V | A | M | T | A | T | P | O | T | R |
| F | L | B | E | T | O | V | E | N | T | A |
| I | A | O | O | E | I | R | O | N | L | O |
| R | V | R | T | S | A | O | T | O | E | O |
| E | A | C | O | F | F | E | E | C | S | U |

BARBECUE  RADIATOR
BONFIRE   SOUP
COCOA     STAR
COFFEE    STEAM
FLAME     STOVE
IRON      SUN
KETTLE    TOAST
LAVA
MAGMA
OVEN
PAN

# WORDS BEGINNING WITH "WH"

```
I  T  A  E  H  W  W  M  E  K  W
E  S  K  S  I  H  W  W  C  H  I
O  W  W  I  H  H  A  I  R  W
W  H  H  T  H  I  H  S  E  H  H
H  W  E  A  R  W  T  H  I  W  I
O  H  R  L  T  L  T  F  W  H  L
L  O  E  K  E  E  F  H  H  A  E
E  O  N  E  H  W  Y  H  E  L  W
H  S  H  W  Z  T  L  E  E  E  H
E  H  I  W  H  E  E  L  Z  H  A
W  H  I  M  P  E  R  E  E  O  M
```

| | |
|---|---|
| WHACK | WHIMPER |
| WHALE | WHIRL |
| WHAM | WHISK |
| WHAT | WHISTLE |
| WHEAT | WHITE |
| WHEEL | WHOLE |
| WHEEZE | WHOOSH |
| WHEN | WHY |
| WHERE | |
| WHETHER | |
| WHIFF | |
| WHILE | |

# ROMAN LIFE

```
C T M Y T H S N I O C
G O T C U D E U Q A F
L G N I R E U Q N O C
A A V T T O A E R D E
D B G I A I M U I S R
I A O E L P M E T O I
A T D S E L T C A L P
T H S R A I A G L D M
O S O T O W N S Y I E
R R C I A S O M O E E
S N T O I R A H C R R
```

AQUEDUCT
BATHS
CHARIOT
CITIES
COINS
CONQUERING
EMPERORS
EMPIRE
FORUM
GLADIATOR
GODS

ITALY
MOSAIC
MYTHS
ROME
SOLDIER
TEMPLE
TOGA
TOWNS
VILLA

# PLAYING A BOARD GAME

**59**

```
                      R P
                      L U L U
    C     E           L A
    T A V E           E Y
    O O R U           S E
    M A K D           R R
    U S R E           P S
D Q S S P I N N E R O C S
S S T A E S I W K C O L C
U T N P S W R O L L I N G
N A I R O E C E I P Y D P
O R O L L D O U B L E S R
B T P E U C O U N T E R S
```

| | |
|---|---|
| BONUS | POINTS |
| CARD | ROLL DOUBLES |
| CLOCKWISE | ROLLING |
| COUNTERS | RULES |
| DICE | SCORE |
| LOSE | SPINNER |
| MOVE | SQUARE |
| PASS | START |
| PIECE | TOKEN |
| PLAYERS | WIN |

# 60

# IT'S ELECTRIC

```
F L O W D I R G A T Y
T T D S P A R K B E G
H N T I U C R I C U R
G W E B S C I V T P E
I C U R I W O O T O N
L L N T R E I L A W E
B B A F R U G T W E R
S T U L T Y C R C R I
S S L S H O C K U H W
E E D E G R A H C S A
J O L T Y R E T T A B
```

| | |
|---|---|
| BATTERY | LIGHT |
| BULB | POWER |
| CHARGE | SHOCK |
| CIRCUIT | SPARK |
| CURRENT | STATIC |
| ENERGY | SURGE |
| FLOW | SWITCH |
| FUSE | VOLT |
| GRID | WATT |
| JOLT | WIRE |

# ALL ABOUT LEAVES

```
S  H  Y  E  L  L  O  W  I  D  E
E  Y  R  D  Y  Y  T  T  O  P  S
T  L  M  N  A  I  I  V  F  M  W
W  F  E  M  Y  H  C  N  U  R  C
O  C  S  G  E  R  T  F  I  N  Y
R  R  Y  H  N  T  L  O  W  R  X
R  I  R  O  I  A  R  O  O  I  A
A  S  R  R  T  N  R  I  N  M  W
N  P  U  R  M  B  Y  O  C  G  S
D  L  F  A  L  L  E  N  Y  A  A
N  E  E  R  G  Y  K  I  P  S  L
```

| | |
|---|---|
| ALIVE | SHINY |
| BROWN | SMOOTH |
| CRISP | SPIKY |
| CRUNCHY | SPOTTY |
| DRY | SYMMETRICAL |
| FALLEN | WAXY |
| FLAT | WIDE |
| FURRY | YELLOW |
| GREEN | |
| LONG | |
| NARROW | |
| ORANGE | |

# 62 DECK OF CARDS

```
O F T A I N K R E K I
W L I B D S I C E C A
T E U V P D E N A N T
I L S A E Q W D E J H
C A D E K C A L B Q R
N E I G H T N E T U E
S E V E N C T D D E E
R U O F D L S E C E J
U J O K E R C R I N A
G N I K U K H E A R T
O T D N O M A I D A E
```

| | |
|---|---|
| ACE | NINE |
| BLACK | QUEEN |
| CLUB | RED |
| DECK | SEVEN |
| DIAMOND | SPADE |
| EIGHT | SUIT |
| FIVE | THREE |
| FOUR | TWO |
| HEART | |
| JACK | |
| JOKER | |
| KING | |

# STILL A WORD WITHOUT ITS FIRST LETTER

**63**

```
K  P  N  C  L  Y  T  R  A  P  L
A  C  H  A  E  P  H  R  G  O  Y
E  G  O  R  P  P  I  W  A  D  A
P  N  E  L  L  S  G  T  R  C  R
S  H  P  U  C  P  H  E  L  S  E
T  C  M  L  W  N  A  O  N  M  P
L  P  L  H  A  D  A  A  V  M  P
R  A  E  P  S  C  I  E  A  E  A
C  R  A  F  T  L  E  L  L  U  R
E  E  L  I  M  S  C  O  L  C  L
O  C  L  O  U  D  K  C  U  L  P
```

| | |
|---|---|
| CLAMP | PLUMP |
| CLEAN | SMILE |
| CLOCK | SNAIL |
| CLOUD | SPAN |
| CRAFT | SPEAK |
| DREAD | SPEAR |
| HOVER | THERE |
| PARTY | THIGH |
| PLACE | TRACE |
| PLUCK | WHERE |

# 64
# "THANK YOU" IN OTHER LANGUAGES

```
H A N D A R I G A T O
V G H P I C R E M D O
A R C O H M E A Z E S
L A L C L K S I T K O
A C O T N A E S A U T
T I I A I K H P K J I
O A D T U U H A K I I
D S A J R I A S M C K
A R E P A L D I E S C
G K A M S I A B K A A
Z E I Z A R G O I E T
```

| | |
|---|---|
| ARIGATO | KAMSIA |
| DANKE | KIITOS |
| DEKUJI | MAHALO |
| DIOLCH | MERCI |
| DZIEKUJE | PALDIES |
| GRACIAS | SPASIBO |
| GRATIAS | TACK |
| GRAZIE | TAKK |
| HVALA | TODA |

# THE WATER CYCLE

```
N  N  N  N  N  T  P  O  F  F  L  N  N
R  O  O  O  O  I  U  N  F  C  O  O  O
T  G  I  I  I  S  O  I  O  A  N  I  I
O  R  T  T  T  N  R  L  N  O  T  T  T
N  O  A  C  A  E  N  O  U  I  A  A  A
L  U  R  E  S  T  E  G  R  T  N  R  R
C  N  I  L  N  O  I  I  E  N  I  O  T
T  D  P  L  E  F  L  P  A  F  A  P  L
A  W  S  O  D  O  S  E  I  I  R  A  I
A  A  N  C  N  N  C  R  W  C  A  V  F
P  T  A  I  O  O  A  N  N  S  E  E  N
F  E  R  U  C  L  O  U  D  S  T  R  I
A  R  T  O  W  T  C  N  T  P  O  I  P
```

CLOUDS
COLLECTION
CONDENSATION
EVAPORATION
GROUNDWATER
INFILTRATION
OCEAN
PRECIPITATION
RAIN

RUN-OFF
TRANSPIRATION

# 66 FOOD FROM GREECE

```
T A S P A N A K O P I T A
T A S D P I Y Y A A R T O
L D R O O A K A S S U O M
A O S A U L S I S E V F T
S A I A M V M T Z A A I S
A B G T F A L A I T A A Y
R A Y S K E S A D T A Z E
A K R I P D T A K E S Z S
O L O D M A A A L I S I T
U A M T L A Y T K A R A O
A V P L U O A K D E T F G
L A U M P D A S A I U A S
L K A U T A S T A U A A T
```

BAKLAVA          SPANAKOPITA
DOLMADES         TARAMASALATA
FETA             TZATZIKI
GYRO
MOUSSAKA
PASTITSIO
SOUVLAKI

# DAIRY PRODUCTS

```
R B U Y S M A E R C E C I
O W U L A O H I T A R Y A
E T H T E A U I A A I O R
M E M I T R K R E C E G T
C I G I P E M P C Y C U E
O E L I M P R T R R E R Y
C T T K A M E R R A E T K
R G A M I T U D O N G A O
G R C L E P W L C M E S M
A C H E E S E I T R W A E
H R M A R G A R I N E A S
M A O E A M R C C A H A O
E I N A I L R E B M E R M
```

BUTTER
CHEESE
GELATO
ICE CREAM
MARGARINE
MILK

SOUR CREAM
WHIPPED CREAM
YOGURT

# KITCHEN TOOLS

68

```
P N E G G P O A C H E R E
B O N E I A D C S P S N U
O E T I R R E X I M S I U
T E B A P U R E T A R G N
T R N L T G T H N U W N R
L S T T E O N G I S H W E
E C G A T N M I P L I G N
O A R N E R D A L N S L I
P L H W O O L E S L K E A
E E A H D T T G R H O L R
N S A H E O R I R N E R T
E A L U T A P S R A O R S
R R E K C A R C T U N E E
```

BLENDER
BOTTLE OPENER
EGG POACHER
GRATER
MIXER
NUTCRACKER
POTATO MASHER
ROLLING PIN
SCALES

SPATULA
STRAINER
TONGS
WHISK

# SLUMBER PARTY

**69**

```
S G T I T B E O L A G P H
G T E E E B P H M S N T S
N E N T K F S I K L R O U
I D N T O N H C H E O O R
R D R R P H A N T E C T B
E Y T A S N S L E P P H H
P B S V S H D N B I O P T
S E E E N E N S N N P A O
I A M L T I E A P G O S O
H R A B I V I D O B L T T
W R G A I O R E I A E E D
S B W G H M F E E G E T G
M I D N I G H T F E A S T
```

BLANKET
FORT
FRIENDS
GAMES
MIDNIGHT FEAST
MOVIE
POPCORN
SLEEPING BAG
SNACKS
TEDDY BEAR
TOOTHBRUSH

TOOTHPASTE
TRAVEL BAG
WHISPERING

# 70 FRUIT JUICES

```
        K R N
        O I
W E A   A   W N P
  E A E A P P L E I I P
  T N A R R U C K C A L B O
  H K P O M E G R A N A T E
  S T R A W B E R R Y W L R
  Y R R E B N A R C A A G E
  C M A N G O P L I M E G P
  E P A T C H E R R Y N E
    G G E P A R G O A A
    O T A M O T R R E
      L E M O N
```

APPLE
BLACKCURRANT
CHERRY
CRANBERRY
GRAPE
KIWI
LEMON
LIME
MANGO
ORANGE

PEAR
POMEGRANATE
STRAWBERRY
TOMATO

# REPTILES

```
N I P A R R E T G K P T R
C H A M E L E O N O L R U
S K I N K P N T E M A U A
T D A L E K A N S O L C S
U R R A T E E C E D T R O
S L O W W O R M I O R O N
O Z I T L I Z A R D N C I
E E I A A G R T R R R O D
L R I G E G O O S A R D R
T E L C U I I T R G I I K
R E K O S A C L T O R L L
U O E E O A N R L N L E A
T N A S G D O A N A N R U
```

ALLIGATOR
CHAMELEON
CROCODILE
DINOSAUR
GECKO
IGUANA
KOMODO
DRAGON

LIZARD
SKINK
SLOWWORM
SNAKE
TERRAPIN
TORTOISE
TURTLE

# 72 VISION TEST

| S | S | E | S | S | A | L | G | D | H | S | A | L |
|---|---|---|---|---|---|---|---|---|---|---|---|---|
| G | N | I | H | T | P | N | B | A | Y | E | P | I |
| N | M | N | A | S | E | O | T | I | Y | S | P | P |
| I | O | U | P | S | O | I | G | E | I | R | O | U |
| D | O | M | E | R | R | S | S | R | R | E | I | P |
| A | R | B | S | A | D | I | I | E | I | T | N | V |
| E | K | E | E | E | G | V | A | E | E | T | T | S |
| R | R | R | U | H | L | Y | T | R | O | E | M | U |
| K | A | S | T | E | N | R | H | S | F | L | E | C |
| N | D | O | N | S | A | R | G | R | T | A | N | O |
| N | T | S | N | O | I | U | I | H | U | A | T | F |
| I | E | R | R | G | R | L | L | R | O | M | L | H |
| S | L | M | T | I | R | B | I | S | E | E | N | Y |

APPOINTMENT
BLURRY VISION
DARK ROOM
EYESIGHT
FOCUS
GLASSES
IRIS
LENSES
LETTERS
LIGHT

NUMBERS
PUPIL
READING
SHAPES

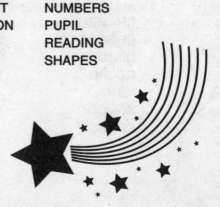

# ON AN ADVENTURE 73

```
I H E E T A T D R E R G I
E U T G M R I H X E P G T
V N T A S R A P L T A S I
H T P Y N U E V R A E U X
C T V O H R O E E U O N P
R O R V I E K I Q L I G O
A R X E R I I U S R U P
E I N N O I T I D E P X E
S C T N D L L N T I I L N
E N L E R J O U R N E Y N
G N I T T O R T E B O L G
A B I T O H E X P L O R E
A M I S S I O N S S L E R
```

EXPEDITION
EXPERIENCE
EXPLORE
GLOBE-TROTTING
GOAL
HUNT
JOURNEY
MISSION
PURSUIT
QUEST
SEARCH

TRAVEL
TREK
TRIP
VOYAGE

# HOUSEPLANTS

```
D R A C A E N A P A S E E
A O R C H I D E N P C T C
H N N A A A A D I H N R A
T D T Y L C A D E A T U M
N Y B H E O E V L P C B A
I P U L U R E P A A T B R
C A I Y P R A V C A H E Y
A L I L I R I T E C A R L
Y Y A A B R U U B R R P L
H N U E C S R A M O A L I
T I Z C Y C L A M E N A S
C N S U C C U L E N T N Y
R A R E C A P A L M U T L
```

ALOE VERA
AMARYLLIS
ANTHURIUM
ARECA PALM
CACTUS
CYCLAMEN
DRACAENA
ECHEVERIA
HYACINTH
ORCHID

PEACE LILY
RUBBER PLANT
SPIDER PLANT
SUCCULENT
YUCCA
ZEBRA PLANT

# YOU CAN SEE THROUGH IT

**75**

**MISSING MIDDLE**

For instructions on how to do this puzzle, turn back to the introduction.

```
L D L A L L B T G E T R E
E E R E U E L W E D R E C
W E R Y A L I D N R C P R
B R N K G N L O B E B A E
W L E L D L M A L G D P L
E R U O I       B G C G E
L R W B I       L B I N N
T E A D T       E C N I S
T T L A H H S V I C E C N
O A G A N S G C I R C A O
B W N S N R L I D L G R I
E E D E A E E G L I O T V
N L A E S U O H N E E R G
```

AIR
BEAKER
BOTTLE
CELLOPHANE
DIAMOND
DRY GLUE
GLASS
GREENHOUSE
ICE
ICICLE
LENS
LIGHT BULB
OLIVE OIL
TRACING PAPER
WATER
WINDOW

# 76

# LOTS OF "B"S

```
O R E B B U L B E H U B W
B B D I U B U B D T R B O
B A H N R B E E N U O C B
E O S B A U B I B O B O B
G B I A B B B U R M A B L
A A R J T B R B H R B W E
B B E A O L R E G E B E B
B T B B R E W B B B L B O
A R B B A G T E R B E B A
C E I E B U L L U A U Y R
A E G R B M G B L L B R D
A B T B T S E I B B O L B
B L U E B E R R Y B U S H
```

| | |
|---|---|
| BABBLE | GIBBERISH |
| BAOBAB TREE | HUBBUB |
| BLABBERMOUTH | JABBER |
| BLOBBIEST | RUBBER BAND |
| BLUBBER | WOBBLE BOARD |
| BLUEBERRY | |
| BUSH | |
| BLURB | |
| BOBBIN | |
| BUBBLEGUM | |
| CABBAGE | |
| COBWEBBY | |

# FORCES AND MOVEMENT

```
A W N N P D Y N A M I C S
E M D T H G I E W I E C S
T I M E H G A R D R G S S
M U T N E M O M U R A P O
N O I S N E T S A M I A P
I Y E M A T S V O N A E I
S I N T I E I P P I I R D
P I N E R T I A N A S T O
E C R P Y T S U R H T E D
E N O I T A R E L E C C A
D N A R E A C T I O N P P
T I A F R I C T I O N M R
T O M A G N E T I S M E T
```

ACCELERATION
DRAG
DYNAMICS
FRICTION
GRAVITY
INERTIA
MAGNETISM
MASS
MOMENTUM
PRESSURE
REACTION

SPEED
SPIN
TENSION
THRUST
TIME
WEIGHT

# PERCUSSION INSTRUMENTS

```
G O N G M B A S S D R U M
A M S L A B M Y C A L G M
R O Y O M A R I M B A L V
S C A S T A N E T S T O I
N A B I N B S L X L E C B
A A C R C E O Y T L H K R
R I I A M O L N G L M E A
E L N I R O W N G O A N P
D N H A P A A B T O E S H
R C L H P I M M E M S P O
U L O A R M O B I L W I N
M N A T H T I I M O L E E
E T S E L E C T S I L L A
```

| | |
|---|---|
| BASS DRUM | MARACAS |
| BONGOS | MARIMBA |
| CASTANETS | SNARE DRUM |
| CELESTE | TIMPANI |
| CHIMES | TOM-TOM |
| COWBELL | TRIANGLE |
| CYMBALS | VIBRAPHONE |
| GLOCKENSPIEL | XYLOPHONE |
| GONG | |

# MEXICAN COOKING

```
F R I J O L E S O J O Q A
S H C B A A A O A G T U T
P A D H A R H T U F O E I
I S T A I C A A A E S S N
C L O S A M C J E M T A R
O A R N A A I F N P A D A
D S T C M T O C C A D I C
E A I O A E T C H N A L A
G N L A M L I A I A A L R
A E L A A A R E L D N A I
L L A O U M R C A A A G O
L D G E O A U M D A F A A
O O A N A T B D A O C A T
```

BURRITO
CARNITA
CHIMICHANGA
EMPANADA
ENCHILADA
FAJITA
FRIJOLES
GUACAMOLE
NACHO
PICO DE GALLO

QUESADILLA
SALSA
TACO
TAMALE
TORTILLA
TOSTADA

# TREEHOUSE FUN

```
T R A P D O O R E P O R A
R W A L K I E T A L K I E
W S S D R O W S S A P A E
M L R A L A D D E R L S S
B E G A L F U O M A C E C
T E L E S C O P E O M H W
D L W W O D N I W A I S P
O R E T L E H S G D E O T
A M D K R S A D E S S R B
B R A N C H R A W T E O O
T R O F T A W I E E M D O
I A D D O A N R C R B K K
E S E B Y G S C O T A E S
```

BOARD GAMES        SWING
BOOKS              TELESCOPE
BRANCH             TRAP DOOR
CAMOUFLAGE         TREE
FORT               WALKIE-TALKIE
HIDEAWAY           WINDOW
LADDER
PASSWORD
POSTERS
ROPE
SHELTER

# PUPPET SHOW

**MISSING MIDDLE**

For instructions on how to do this puzzle, turn back to the introduction.

```
T D S C H A R A C T E R C
F S G N I R T S P D E D I
I C P O U N P S N R N E T
N I U P R E C D S U C N N
G S A P E E A S O N W V E
E U P C N       A C U R M
R M H E C       S H R L E
P F R E G       P I G I V
U Y W E C O I C O S L G O
P M R A F R E R R W O H M
P I B R P O P I P I V T R
E B E C S R T P E R E S C
T P H C N U P T L E S M T
```

BACKGROUND
CHARACTER
DANCE
FINGER PUPPET
GLOVES
LIGHTS
MOVEMENT
MUSIC
PERFORMANCE
PROPS

PUNCH
SCENERY
SCRIPT
SPEECH
STAGE
STRING
WIRE

# 82 WORDS FROM GREEK

```
I T T C T E Y X A L A G H
G E A O C L I E R R L C P
E L S T E B A H P L A T A
O E A M T U E C H O E N R
G V N E I I R R G N H P G
R I A R H C C O A A H M O
A S I U C I R L P A P U T
P I B A R T P O R E I S O
H O I S A A N M S S A I H
Y N H O G S A I H C M C P
P A P N T C P A A T O O C
P A M I Y R E T A R C P M
B P A D T E L E P H O N E
```

ALPHABET          MICROSCOPE
AMPHIBIAN         MUSIC
ARCHITECT         PHARMACY
ATTIC                  PHOTOGRAPH
CRATER              PLANET
DINOSAUR          TELEPHONE
ECHO                  TELEVISION
EUROPE
GALAXY
GEOGRAPHY

# FRACTIONS 83

```
H T F L E W T H R A E H A
D R I H T E I H D I E T T
H H V L T D F T G H E D H
N T T S I X T H T T H E T
S E N N S I T G E T N R N
I T L E E H I N T I D E
X T T E E E V E E D N N E
T H H N V T T E H N T U T
E E T H N E F N N A H H R
E H F T H T N I E T L V U
N T I E E T H T F V H F O
T N F X I E E T H N E H F
H E I R E T R A U Q T S N
```

EIGHTEENTH

EIGHTH

ELEVENTH

FIFTEENTH

FIFTH

FOURTEENTH

HALF

HUNDREDTH

NINTH

QUARTER

SEVENTEENTH

SEVENTH

SIXTEENTH

SIXTH

TENTH

THIRD

TWELFTH

# CLEANING EQUIPMENT

**84**

```
S T N A T C E F N I S I D
M A I R F R E S H E N E R
H S I L O P D S R P A A L
R P R V D R U U H T O L C
H S U R B I S T S P R A Y
I C R L E I T D D S E G U
P O M E F U P M P S L I V
V D R I A S A O P O E A S
B U C K E T N M V A C A D
S A E P W G I E O U O E P
I C S A E E S U U O G S N
M U X G R T C M E A R S S
D A P G N I R U O C S B A
```

AIR FRESHENER
BROOM
BRUSH
BUCKET
CLOTH
DISINFECTANT
DUSTPAN
GLOVES
MOP

POLISH
SCOURING PAD
SOAP
SPONGE
SPRAY
VACUUM
WAX

# IT'S A ROOM

| | | | | | | | | | | | | |
|---|---|---|---|---|---|---|---|---|---|---|---|---|
| O | C | E | M | O | O | R | S | S | A | L | C | T |
| M | O | O | R | H | T | A | B | T | R | H | L | T |
| O | O | F | F | I | C | E | H | A | A | I | E | M |
| M | D | U | M | C | I | A | L | N | V | T | O | C |
| N | I | G | F | K | L | L | G | I | N | O | G | L |
| E | N | N | D | L | E | I | N | E | R | D | B | O |
| H | I | M | R | C | N | G | M | Y | T | T | E | A |
| C | N | A | T | G | R | E | T | A | E | M | D | K |
| T | G | Y | R | O | S | I | A | T | S | O | R | R |
| I | R | O | O | A | L | O | C | T | T | T | O | O |
| K | O | M | B | I | S | S | A | I | U | O | O | O |
| M | O | R | T | R | R | O | M | C | D | Y | M | M |
| G | M | U | T | L | R | O | E | O | Y | T | R | E |

ATTIC
BASEMENT
BATHROOM
BEDROOM
CELLAR
CHANGING ROOM
CLASSROOM
CLOAKROOM
DINING ROOM
HALL

KITCHEN
LIVING ROOM
OFFICE
STUDY
UTILITY ROOM

# 86 THINGS THAT GLOW

```
B E A C O N R E I E E R R
T R T O R M R T G S F B S
E E O F E A N S U E L T E
S B R A T U I O L U F E I
J M C S A R H D B K I L A
E E H E E T N T C I R E R
L E D L H A H I S T E V O
L L T G C G T I R L F I R
Y A I L I S I F D T L S U
F L O L W E M A L F Y I A
I N R O E R I F N O B O G
S D L H S I F R E L G N A
H G F S P A R K D N L V B
```

ANGLERFISH          JELLYFISH
AURORA              LED
BEACON              LIGHTBULB
BONFIRE             LIGHTHOUSE
CANDLE              SPARK
EMBER               STAR
FIREFLY             TELEVISION
FLAME               TORCH
GLOW STICK
HEATER

# CONSTELLATIONS

```
S U N G Y C S U E S R E P
O N C M S N E A M U I C A
R E S U R U A T N E C A N
R A L M H G N N U A S S S
O C A N I S M I N O R S N
N S R G O A O I H J R I O
I E B H O R S U O P J O C
M C I S I M U Y U A L P A
A S L O A J A R D Y H E R
S I N J G O G R I V O I D
R P O A D E M O R D N A S
U R P E G A S U S P U A B
N R U U R O J A M A S R U
```

ANDROMEDA
CANIS MAJOR
CANIS MINOR
CASSIOPEIA
CENTAURUS
CYGNUS
DELPHINUS
DRACO
HYDRA
LEO
LIBRA

ORION
PEGASUS
PERSEUS
PISCES
URSA MAJOR
URSA MINOR
VIRGO

# CODING

```
C B R D I S P L A Y T N O
I I O N O I T C N U F R U
T L U C A L G O R I T H M
E A R T N L C I G O L C C
M N T N T O I L N G E G M
H G N E U V I P O A M N A
T U E M P O A T R O T I R
I A M N N L U R I P P R G
R G U G I U A T I D O T O
A E G I U Y R R P A N S R
S I R S C A C P T U B O P
U L A S G S L H H G T L C
D L E A O P E R A T O R E
```

ALGORITHM          LOGIC
ARGUMENT           LOOP
ARITHMETIC         OPERATOR
ARRAY              OUTPUT
ASSIGNMENT         PROGRAM
CONDITION          RUN
DISPLAY            SCRIPT
FUNCTION           STRING
INPUT              VARIABLE
LANGUAGE

# FLOWER ARRANGING

**89**

```
E M R B L B O U Q U E T P
I G P S E W L V T B G A T
G R T A A R A E I O R T F
A E Y N V S T T F W C O L
R E I P E R R G R U M S O
L N N P S I E E T W F T R
A E G B M R P I G N O E I
N R L M I A I I A I O M S
D Y I B P N R I L W D S T
G N B R G P S L A T E P N
G O G A S R E W O L F T D
N P L A S T I C W R A P N
S T R I S P R A Y R N E N
```

BOUQUET

CUTTING

FLORIST

FLOWERS

FOOD

GARLAND

GREENERY

LEAVES

PAPER WRAP

PETALS

PLASTIC WRAP

RIBBON

SPRAY

SPRIG

STEMS

TRIMMING

TYING

VASE

WATER

# 90 FOOD CHAIN

```
T O U E R O V I B R E H S
N P E S U N M A Y L R C E
A R R R R A P H A E A A C
L E O E C E A M U V R N O
P D V S X A I R E N O P S
R A I O S N R N C T T R Y
O T N P A U G N K S C E S
D O M M A E G N I P H T T
U R O O R N A N T V F A E
C S U C A L V M U T O W M
E T P E P T R P A F Y R N
R Y A D R E M U S N O C E
O R T A T I B A H H A B O
```

ANIMAL
APEX
CARNIVORE
CONSUMER
DECOMPOSER
ECOSYSTEM
FUNGUS
HABITAT
HERBIVORE
HUNT
OMNIVORE

PLANKTON
PLANT
PREDATOR
PREY
PRODUCER
SCAVENGER
SUN
WATER

# THINGS WITH STRIPES 91

```
B G A L F K N U M P I H C
B E E B E L B M U B L S E
A L I C C A U N I F O R M
R T L L A Z N O G T B A N
C I T A E N F R N K N E M
O B A B B B D I E T C U K
D A R H Y L M Y A G B R P
E A R P C R O C C H D S K
A C C E E K Y O S A Z A D
F B K P G B C P P K N B B
T B P R B I S E M N U E P
B E I A A A T D D N P N U
P O T B W C R I P A K O K
```

BADGER
BARCODE
BUMBLEBEE
CANDY CANE
CHIPMUNK
DECKCHAIR
FLAG
OKAPI
PEPPERMINT
POOL BALL
SKUNK

TABBY CAT
TIGER
UNIFORM
WASP
ZEBRA

# ON THE ROAD

**92**

```
N P C S C V O C L A N E F
F G O O S O R I I C O R R
V B I T R O N G N R V E S
R P A S S N N E T E E V T
I R H S P S E A E F H O R
O O I O N O U R R L I C E
E N V O I T T B S E C E E
G F S V G R E S E C L L T
G N I K R A P I C T E O L
S A G S O F E S T O T H I
S E N I L F R S I R P N G
N I A R D I A I O S T A H
R O L D O C R O N F V M T
```

BUS STOP
CONE
CORNER
CROSSING
DRAIN
INTERSECTION
LANE
LINES
MANHOLE COVER

PARKING
REFLECTORS
SIGNAL
STOP SIGN
STREET LIGHT
TRAFFIC
VEHICLE

# MODEL TRAIN SET

```
M N O I T A T S A E A L E
I R E I H C T I W S O L G
P N O O N I R I T C R S D
A G R F I N I E O R I R I
S E L R T D G M I T N O R
S N A A A A O A R R H N B
E G D O N T L A C L R L E
N I R S I G C P A V O A C
G N U V N K I E R A M P B
E E E F G N I S S O R C E
R P C O N T R O L L E R T
O G R A C R D R R A I L T
I O T M A T U N N E L D E
```

| | |
|---|---|
| BARRIER | SIGNAL |
| BRIDGE | STATION |
| CARGO | SWITCH |
| CONTROLLER | TRACK |
| CROSSING | TUNNEL |
| ENGINE | |
| LOCOMOTIVE | |
| PASSENGER | |
| PLATFORM | |
| RAIL | |
| RAMP | |
| ROAD | |

# 94 NORTHERN HEMISPHERE COUNTRIES

**MISSING MIDDLE** For instructions on how to do this puzzle, turn back to the introduction.

```
A I E H O N D U R A S M P
I N P T A P A C A I O P N
D I A N H B A T E N G I M
N A K A U I P N G M L G D
I O I C         A I G O
I G S D         M U M D
O E T E         A A O N
C R A S         A T R A
I M N U         N N O L
X A E A E A M N Y A A C O
E N N I O A I O I N P C P
M Y V M L V A N M F A O C
P P A A D A N A C N J R M
```

| | |
|---|---|
| CANADA | JAPAN |
| CHINA | MALI |
| CUBA | MEXICO |
| EGYPT | MONGOLIA |
| ETHIOPIA | MOROCCO |
| FINLAND | PAKISTAN |
| GERMANY | PANAMA |
| GUATEMALA | POLAND |
| HONDURAS | SPAIN |
| INDIA | VIETNAM |

# ORIGAMI

```
C B C R E A S E N T R E E
P U E J C O N S T R U C T
R N B N C I R T E M O E G
I I U E D E U V X O B N D
T A U R E E S O A T T E L
I T T U R C O E L L C M I
R N H L A I R R N O L F L
O U G E U T V E R A O E S
P O I R Q M F A A L P T Y
A M A T S E T A D T A A S
P T R E A I R A R R E L J
E C T M O D E L C C C T A
R O S N E R E S I C E R P
```

| | |
|---|---|
| BEND | MODEL |
| BOX | MOUNTAIN |
| CONSTRUCT | PAPER |
| CRAFT | PRECISE |
| CREASE | RULER |
| CREATE | SQUARE |
| CUBE | STAR |
| DECORATION | STRAIGHT |
| FOLD | VALLEY |
| GEOMETRIC | |
| JAPANESE | |

96

# COMIC STRIP

```
R E T C A R A H C R I C Y
N X C T N O O L L A B E R
T A C R O T S P E E C H O
S S R C I T S C E N E P T
D N I R T P N B T O A O S
R E O T A T E O R I R I O
A E T I R T W X B T E N X
W R X A T A I U P P P T I
I U E O S C B O N A A E U
N T T E U B A R N C P R E
G C S I L S T H G U O H T
I I I E L C I M O C A O E
A P I T I E A G N A M T A
```

ACTION
ARTIST
BALLOON
BOX
BUBBLE
CAPTION
CHARACTER
COMIC
DRAWING
ILLUSTRATION
MANGA
NARRATION

PAPER
PICTURE
POINTER
SCENE
SPEECH
STORY
TEXT
THOUGHTS

# VOLCANOES

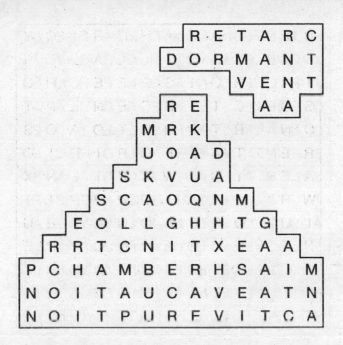

```
                    R E T A R C
                  D O R M A N T
                            V E N T
                          A A
            R E
          M R K
          U O A D
        S K V U A
      S C A O Q N M
    E O L L G H H T G
  R R T C N I T X E A A
P C H A M B E R H S A I M
N O I T A U C A V E A T N
N O I T P U R F V I T C A
```

| | |
|---|---|
| ACTIVE | GAS |
| ASH | HEAT |
| CHAMBER | LAVA |
| CLOUD | MAGMA |
| CRATER | MOUNTAIN |
| DORMANT | PRESSURE |
| EARTHQUAKE | ROCK |
| ERUPTION | VENT |
| EVACUATION | |
| EXTINCT | |

# 98 MADE OF STONE

```
H T N E M U N O M A E E S
I O B P A V I N G G S Y J
T R O F O N N U N E R M E
O B E L I S K E R C D A W
O B A F I A H U E E I D E
E E N N A E T N L C M C L
S N B A N P O A O B A A S
T C I O L T I B C R R S R
A H T U S D B A L S Y T A
T S C E N L U R R O P L L
U S L U E R E K R A M E L
E I S S E N I R H S J Y I
M T N I F O U N T A I N P
```

| | |
|---|---|
| BENCH | OBELISK |
| CASTLE | PAVING |
| COBBLES | PILLAR |
| DAM | PYRAMID |
| FORT | SCULPTURE |
| FOUNTAIN | SHRINE |
| JEWELS | SLAB |
| MARKER | STATUE |
| MILESTONE | STONEHENGE |
| MONUMENT | SUNDIAL |

# SPACESHIP

**99**

```
F N C O N W O D T N U O C
B N A I R L O C K K C O D
S P O E E L A U N C H O K
P P S I G N D R S L U F D
I S A N S S G L A T G G B
L C I C I S O I E D R K L
O W L G E R I R N A I H A
T O N A T W S M V E A O S
S A R N L P A I A T T N T
L E O B A I T L C N H T O
D C A C I Y O H K A C B F
C A E T K T R O C K E T F
S F I G N I T I O N T G N
```

AIRLOCK

BLAST OFF

CONTROLS

COUNTDOWN

DOCK

ENGINE

GRAVITY

HATCH

IGNITION

LAUNCH

MISSION

ORBIT

OUTER SPACE

PILOT

RADIO

ROCKET

SEAT

SIGNAL

SPACEWALK

WING

# 100 EUROPEAN CITIES

**MISSING MIDDLE** For instructions on how to do this puzzle, turn back to the introduction.

```
R V A L L E T T A O S L O
S R V D B U C H A R E S T
T E A I I I R E U G A R P
O A R V O K Z A G R E B L
C O M W         L A T J
K A O S         B O N U
H N V V         S T A B
O V E I         L H C L
L I J L         E E M J
M E A N I N D D W A H H A
S N R I N R L N A W R T N
N N A U S E I A O M G B A
N A S S K B R B N L S R A
```

| | |
|---|---|
| AMSTERDAM | OSLO |
| ATHENS | PRAGUE |
| BERN | SARAJEVO |
| BRATISLAVA | STOCKHOLM |
| BUCHAREST | TALLINN |
| HELSINKI | VALLETTA |
| LISBON | VIENNA |
| LJUBLJANA | VILNIUS |
| LONDON | WARSAW |
| MINSK | ZAGREB |

# SPY WORDS

```
R D E C R Y P T M M R I S
E Y M E N E A I P A E S I
T C P E S A S E S T V E T
S O N R G S S E E O N R
A D O E I T I I E R C C O
M M N O G G E G V C R R P
Y I N H N I A S D E E Y S
P R E M A K L E S S D P S
S A E D C N V L L A N T A
S N A A O I D M E T U I P
T R P N C C S L E T M O A
I C R E H P I C E U N N S
E G A N O I P S E R L I E
```

| | |
|---|---|
| AGENT | HANDLER |
| ASSET | INTELLIGENCE |
| ASSIGNMENT | MISSION |
| CIPHER | MORSE |
| CODE | PACKAGE |
| DECRYPT | PASSPORT |
| DEVICE | SECRET |
| ENCRYPTION | SPYMASTER |
| ENEMY | UNDERCOVER |
| ESPIONAGE | VISA |

# THINGS THAT ARE SMALL

```
P  I  E  C  E  O  F  G  R  A  V  E  L
I  R  A  I  N  D  R  O  P  P  C  G  S
D  B  U  T  T  O  N  T  E  F  E  R  P
E  N  O  L  E  N  T  I  L  R  P  A  L
F  D  A  T  E  T  R  E  E  E  C  I  I
E  I  S  S  T  N  L  R  P  C  N  N  N
G  A  D  L  F  L  A  P  T  K  I  O  T
D  M  A  P  D  O  E  A  U  L  S  F  E
E  O  T  I  B  R  N  C  N  E  I  R  R
E  N  I  E  C  E  C  I  A  T  A  I  D
S  D  A  O  O  R  E  O  A  P  R  C  A
U  N  R  M  F  D  C  O  I  R  A  E  E
L  N  N  E  E  D  L  E  C  N  G  D  B
```

| | |
|---|---|
| ANT | NEEDLE |
| BEAD | NUT |
| BEAN | PEA |
| BOTTLE CAP | PEPPERCORN |
| BUTTON | PIECE OF GRAVEL |
| COIN | RAINDROP |
| DIAMOND | RAISIN |
| FRECKLE | SEED |
| GRAIN OF RICE | SPLINTER |
| GRAIN OF SAND | |
| LENTIL | |

# GEOMETRY

```
E D I S A E N R E N R O C
R R E N M E A S U R E A A
H G G B O A S S R S E M O
V L E M R E C E L M R N O
E G E P P L T U O M O O B
R P U G A E E Y T L T G T
T I C E M H R L E E A Y U
E R N I C T S F L P T L S
X I R I E E I E A E O E
L E A M P O I N T C R P P
P M M U N I T S N B T A R
B Y Y M I R R O R S O G P
S I G M I R S E G M E N T
```

ACUTE
ANGLE
CORNER
LINE
MEASURE
MIRROR
OBTUSE
PARALLEL
PERFECT
PERIMETER

POINT
POLYGON
ROTATE
SEGMENT
SHAPE
SIDE
SYMMETRY
UNITS
VERTEX

# DINOSAURS

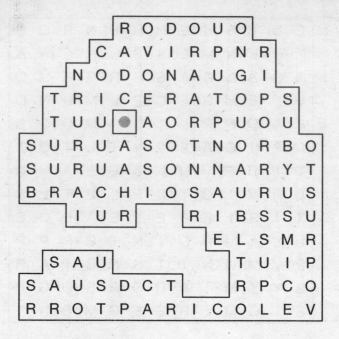

```
      R O D O U O
      C A V I R P N R
      N O D O N A U G I
      T R I C E R A T O P S
      T U U · A O R P U O U
    S U R U A S O T N O R B O
    S U R U A S O N N A R Y T
    B R A C H I O S A U R U S
        I U R     R I B S S U
                  E L S M R
    S A U           T U I P
  S A U S D C T     R P C O
  R R O T P A R I C O L E V
```

**BRACHIOSAURUS**
**BRONTOSAURUS**
**IGUANODON**
**PTEROSAUR**
**TRICERATOPS**
**TYRANNOSAURUS**
**VELOCIRAPTOR**

# MADE WITH TOMATOES

```
L A A A S M G A Z P A C H O O
N N K P S S E C U G O A T R S
H A U A S L A S C P T E O N E
C A H S E S T T S T C D A A C
I O S O Z O B O E U O E S A O
W R K H S O Z H A M B I P L A
D D A A U A C S O D U R L B T
N P H L A S A P E C E A O P A
A L S T U Z L K A S G L U W S
S L A R Z A A A E E O H L U S
T A B I A B E S D G C A K S A
L E P T C A A O N T H L P A P
B C S L U L C E E S E E O L L
E A C S A I S K H A S S C E S
P A T D P E S T C T S A A A U
```

| | |
|---|---|
| BAKED BEANS | PIZZA SAUCE |
| BLT SANDWICH | SALSA |
| BOLOGNESE | SHAKSHUKA |
| BRUSCHETTA | |
| CAPRESE SALAD | |
| GAZPACHO | |
| KETCHUP | |
| PASSATA | |
| PASTA AL POMODORO | |
| PICO DE GALLO | |

```
R S A S I A A S P P M A D A M
S S E N V E L O P E L I A M I
B O H P A R G A R A P S H R S
Y O U R S S I N C E R E L Y M
R A R I E E R U T A N G I S R
R D O B E S T W I S H E S R I
N A I A A E H S D U R N R O N
D T E A M R E N M S R A L E A
E E A A R A E I P I P H S R A
A R N E S P Y I I S T V S T S U
R P P E I S K A E T S T A A R
R A S T H A N K Y O U M M N Y
P N L I D E N N E I R M P R D
N W Y E M P A A D D R E S S N
E S N E S M R P T S H P N U I
```

ADDRESS            SIGNATURE
BEST WISHES        SIR
DATE               STAMP
DEAR               THANK YOU
ENVELOPE           YOURS SINCERELY
MADAM
MAIL
NAME
PAPER
PARAGRAPH
PEN

# WHY I DIDN'T DO MY HOMEWORK

**107**

```
E F L I C O U L D N T D O I T
E R O E O T T N A W T N D I D
M I K R F M O E I K M D D R E
I E O B G T D F R T O E E E K
T N O L T O I I F G M P T T O
E D B E O B T T A M A O N A R
V T Y W O O I T A P O L W W B
A O M A O C E J O T T L I N R
H O T W B I R N C D H T O I E
T K S A T E D A A D O O W L T
N I O Y T A E N T K G I M L U
D T L N H O I N L E U K T E P
I E I D E I D T E L B A T F M
D R E M I T F O T U O N A R O
P L T I K O O T R E T S I S C
```

BLEW AWAY
COMPUTER BROKE
COULDN'T DO IT
DIDN'T HAVE TIME
DIDN'T WANT TO
DOG ATE IT
FELL IN WATER
FORGOT TO DO IT
FRIEND TOOK IT
HAD NO PAPER
LEFT IT AT HOME

LOST MY BOOK
PRINTER JAMMED
RAN OUT OF TIME
SISTER TOOK IT
TABLET DIED

# SOUTHERN HEMISPHERE COUNTRIES

```
Z I M B A B W E P O C A O O U
B N T T A A U A N H A D I N P
I M C G T N R O I A N C F G A
N H O N B A I L N A A D L C P
A L I Z G N E T L T T T I O U
C A M U A I A A N A O R Y U A
S A A A R M E M A E F S R I N
A Y L S L Z B I I A G U E N E
G M R O W A L I H B G R E L W
A A A E G A W T Q U I B A U G
D S N G R N U I A U A A Y I U
A U N T A O A Y M A E A A M I
M Z S A S T A N Z A N I A I N
Z U A I V I L O B N R N A A E
A B O T S W A N A I I W L A A
```

ANGOLA
ARGENTINA
AUSTRALIA
BOLIVIA
BOTSWANA
CHILE
LESOTHO
MADAGASCAR
MALAWI
MOZAMBIQUE
NAMIBIA
NEW ZEALAND
PAPUA NEW
GUINEA
PARAGUAY
SOUTH AFRICA
TANZANIA
URUGUAY
ZIMBABWE

# 109 DECORATING A CAKE

```
P D B S A W A C F E R F E S I
G T R E P A P E L B I D E P M
A N E L P F G T L L I P R I A
B A P K G E L M T B M A E H E
G D N N R R T I L D I L W C R
N N E I E S E E N D R E O E C
I O A R P R G L L N R T L T R
P F E P S L F E R A O T F A E
I A N S I O M M I T R E E L T
P D F T O Z I A W S G K L O T
B N T D I I R R S E L N B C U
E E D I C W R A P K A I I O B
R Y I I N O D C M A Z F D H G
E F N B F R U I T C E E E C M
D G E F R O S T I N G W S E W
```

| | |
|---|---|
| BUTTERCREAM | FRUIT |
| CAKE STAND | ICING |
| CARAMEL | MARZIPAN |
| CHOCOLATE CHIPS | MIRROR GLAZE |
| EDIBLE FLOWER | PALETTE KNIFE |
| EDIBLE GLITTER | PIPING BAG |
| EDIBLE PAPER | SPRINKLES |
| FONDANT | SWIRL |
| FOOD DYE | TIERS |
| FROSTING | WAFERS |

# AT THE OLYMPICS

```
E S T B R S N M U L Y G T I Z
C V T I R O O A M M N E A L A
D O T A M O T D N T O U R A I
I L M P R I N A D M M L R D B
M E W P L T N Z T E E E E E R
E A I M E L U G E N R R G M F
T O N R E T A N T H E M O L S
N E N N A T I N U E C M A L P
E R E V L I S T I O A G M L I
V H R A Y M D P O F N O E O M
E C O U N T R Y O R R L S T C
S C O R E P A E D R R M E M I
O T A M U I D A T S T A D E N
Q U A L I F I E R O M C G P E
E V O L M U I D O P Z R I O O
```

| | |
|---|---|
| ANTHEM | QUALIFIER |
| BRONZE | SCORE |
| CEREMONY | SILVER |
| COMMENTATOR | SPORT |
| COMPETITOR | STADIUM |
| COUNTRY | START |
| EVENT | TEAM |
| FINAL | TIMING |
| FLAG | WINNER |
| MEDAL | |
| PODIUM | |

# TWO DOUBLE LETTERS

**111**

**MISSING MIDDLE** For instructions on how to do this puzzle, turn back to the introduction.

```
E E F F O C T B L F O S E R O
R B T L F R O A L M Z V M S F
O E C R G V F L A A O O B A F
H W P R S D F L B T O L A M I
A O B P M S E O T T K L R O C
P R I K O         E E R O I
P R N I A         E Y A R A
I A N L C         P B S S L
N B K N L         E A S S L
E L E E O         R L O A Y
S E E A U O P D R R N L M L R
S E P N A A S S D E G I E C K
S H E I S T A S S E S E U N A
O W R O T F I H A I S S E M O
S N O O C C A R D B M S E P Z
```

ADDRESS
BALLOON
BASSOON
CLASSROOM
COFFEE
EMBARRASS
FOOTBALL
GODDESS
GRASSHOPPER
HAPPINESS

INNKEEPER
MATTRESS
MILLENNIUM
MISSPELL
OFFICIALLY
RACCOON
TOFFEE
VOLLEYBALL
WHEELBARROW
ZOOKEEPER

# TREASURE MAP

```
A S T H N O I T A C O L G I D
E R N O I P L I C O M P A S S
Y R E R P D I A J R T S A E K
M I T U S S I A K P T R E E L
J V R M L E E N C E R T S S L
E E T D Y C T H G P A P E R O
W R R T I S S A T P O D O O T
E E E L O R T L N S L H D R H
L G A H A O E E E I K A X N T
S O S L E P A C R R D R C O R
E L U H T U O S T Y P R A E O
H D R E C T E R O I M R O M N
I T E S L T R A I L O H H O X
O L K M O N H I L L O N O T C
E R R D C C T M E T L E S H A
```

| | |
|---|---|
| CLUE | NORTH |
| COMPASS | PAPER |
| COORDINATES | RIVER |
| DIG LOCATION | SOUTH |
| DIRECTIONS | TRAIL |
| EAST | TREASURE |
| GOLD | TREE |
| HIDING PLACE | X MARKS THE SPOT |
| HILL | |
| JEWELS | |
| LAKE | |
| MYSTERY | |

# 113 ABOUT GYMNASTICS

```
R D T I E I P O S T U R E S G
N A M L R L S E L I T L U A V
P R M N U T B N B S T G E T D
T L R G R A A M W R M N C S L
S R L E N G S I U C A I N I S
S T T O I I N R U T E D A W P
S C L L R G R R E M B N L T A
H A I P I P M P R M L A A J S
L T A I N N I H S P O L B U R
Y R L U G Z E L N D L S S M I
P A T I S N R P F R N O G P U
R L E E H W T R A C T A T T R
P A R A L L E L B A R S H R L
L H O R I Z O N T A L B A R T
S P O M M E L H O R S E E C U
```

| | |
|---|---|
| AGILITY | POMMEL HORSE |
| BALANCE | POSTURE |
| BEAM | RINGS |
| CARTWHEEL | ROLL |
| FLIP | SOMERSAULT |
| HANDSPRING | STRETCH |
| HORIZONTAL BAR | SWING |
| JUMP | TUMBLE |
| LANDING | TWIST |
| PARALLEL BARS | VAULT |

```
      O C S D R S G
      S R C S L I E L L
    D A K O G I O G B L A
    L N A L C N L M O G M A S
G E A R C H I T E C T I I W S
N S T H G I L R C E M E N T E
I S         I M B       G L
R G         E N C       I B
O N         C S I       W A
O I R F T S A L P L A N S I C
L B U L F O U N D A T I O N S
F M     I R     E K     D N
T U     A S     S P     O G
N L     U G     A I     W S
P P I P E S     D O O R S F
```

**ARCHITECT**
**BRICKS**
**CABLES**
**CEILINGS**
**CEMENT**
**CRANE**
**DIGGING**
**DOORS**
**FLOORING**
**FOUNDATIONS**
**GLASS**

**LIGHTS**
**PIPES**
**PLANS**
**PLASTER**
**PLUMBING**
**TIMBER**
**TOOLS**
**WALLS**
**WINDOWS**

# 115 ALL ABOUT SNAKES

```
A H T E T E D E A O I K E N I
C R I T G E R E H T I L S R L
A S O S S N E O R I G I I F I
E D N E S H A A V N V E I C N
A E R C L K L F U C G I O R C
L T L I O C I J B I G N P E V
I A R C V L L N E I S E E E O
L A T A S K D E R T H L T L R
I E M R L H R B R E T I I A L
A U O N O L E I L T P P E C T
T G N I R C C D A O E T C S E
K N E V L T E R E S O M I T E
C O V O O E N I H L L D I L L
E T L R T H O U N L O B E R E
T S T E S E R P E N T N S D S
```

| | |
|---|---|
| BITE | REPTILE |
| CARNIVORE | SCALE |
| COIL | SERPENT |
| COLD-BLOODED | SHED |
| CONSTRICTOR | SKIN |
| DESERT | SLITHER |
| FANG | TAIL |
| HISS | TONGUE |
| JUNGLE | VENOM |
| RATTLE | VIPER |

# THE VIKINGS

```
R E R A F A E S E T N L Q P R
P T P O F S H I E L D T C I D
D C F M S F T A Q R N V N R O
H E O S A E I R H E A O G A R
M E T N N R U E M C E Y S T R
I R L A Q N A E R I I A C E A
L C D M E U L U N C E G A R N
N C H S E T E R D N E E N O O
R C H I T T E S V E O R D I I
A T N E E D A R T M R S I R T
E R S C I F M E S R O N N R A
P R T A I I T E U V I O A A R
S P R G I S O A N E S A V W G
T H T I S E M P I R E A I R I
P I H S G N O L E N C H A R M
```

CHIEFTAIN
CONQUEST
DANE
EMPIRE
FIERCE
HELMET
LONGSHIP
MARAUDER
MIGRATION
NORSE
PIRATE

RAIDER
RUNES
SCANDINAVIA
SEAFARER
SETTLEMENT
SHIELD
SPEAR
VOYAGER
WARRIOR

# 117 IT ENDS WITH "O"

```
O U O A L C O O O O G N I B A
A N M B U O N L D O G A O L O
J O I C V I T C A M I M E R O
O O K C M D A O A F Q R B A T
K O G O C I M R R L F O O O A
O A D N N U O O O N Y U H G M
H F N D I T P A S L A P B O O
O E I G A M R P O Q U D S N T
R G S T A O A A A H U N O O O
O A O V A R O L O C E I R A L
A P A L A N O L F O B L T A L
O T N I D L G O S Q O A L O E
O E D I V P D O A O N N N O C
O A R M A D I L L O I L P J B
C M O R S H A M P O O A O L O
```

| | |
|---|---|
| ARMADILLO | HELLO |
| BANJO | INDIGO |
| BINGO | KANGAROO |
| BUFFALO | MOSQUITO |
| CALYPSO | POTATO |
| CAPPUCCINO | SHAMPOO |
| CELLO | TANGO |
| CUCKOO | TOMATO |
| DOMINO | TORNADO |
| FLAMINGO | VIDEO |

# LANDLOCKED COUNTRIES

MISSING MIDDLE

For instructions on how to do this puzzle, turn back to the introduction.

```
M L A A A A A O S K E R U B F
A R M E N I A U A A A L A A G
L O E A B I R Z Z D D I N L S
A H U R R A A E E N P A A E E
W Z E T L K R F A O T R A G A
I S S E H . . . . R U R Λ Λ
A U B S A . . . . H U N I A
A A T I N . . . . O M B U A
A A J U Z . . . . O M A L O
N A R T B . . . . A H A D H
N U I U G Z G E D Z I A R V T
B W W F A A X O U G A N D A O
S A A A R U V T C B A L W A S
A B R Y L A B O T S W A N A E
E W B A B M I Z X N E M A A L
```

| | |
|---|---|
| AFGHANISTAN | KAZAKHSTAN |
| ANDORRA | LESOTHO |
| ARMENIA | LUXEMBOURG |
| AUSTRIA | MALAWI |
| AZERBAIJAN | MOLDOVA |
| BELARUS | SERBIA |
| BOTSWANA | SWITZERLAND |
| BURUNDI | UGANDA |
| ETHIOPIA | ZAMBIA |
| HUNGARY | ZIMBABWE |

# TRIP TO THE THEME PARK

119

```
R E E B H T L E B Y T E F A S
L W C O P L I A R O N O M R E
L A H A A G E M I N I G O L F
R I A T R O A L L E I L I E F
E T R I G K R L H F L E D E B
P I A N O A W M T E M I R L U
I N C G T R R S R A R R E S M
H L T L O T H C G P I S O I P
S I E A H O O E U S U U W R E
E N R K P A D C W O V P M E R
T E E E S A A H R E W S E I C
A A B T C E E A N K L N O K A
R I E R T E C I Y A W L I A R
I R A F L E R E C N A R T N E
P N E S U O H D E T N U A H O
```

ARCADE GAME
BOATING LAKE
BUMPER CAR
CAROUSEL
CHARACTER
ENTRANCE
FERRIS WHEEL
GIFT SHOP
GO-KART
HAUNTED HOUSE
MINIGOLF

MONORAIL
PHOTOGRAPH
PIRATE SHIP
RAILWAY
ROLLER COASTER
SAFETY BELT
SOUVENIR
TEACUP RIDE
WAIT IN LINE

# FAMILY TREE

```
E R N T E A R E H T O M R A E
T O M N D E V I T A L E R P T
A T R A E E C S I R C E H O N
I S A D H T V E B O E O T A A
D E Y N R N R O R R T T U A T
E C C E E E N D M O O R S E Y
M N O C H R E M G E E T E I T
M A U S T A T R A E R D H Y S
I R S E A P A H L R L E O E O
I C I D F P E C T I R U C E R
E T N L H A N H H M N I O N R
R S E N C U N C R G E I A E O
V E H C R A E S E R R S G G A
Y R O T S I H R T O B C R T E
S N O I T A R E N E G A S I O
```

ANCESTOR
BROTHER
CHILD
COUSIN
DESCENDANT
FATHER
GENERATION
HISTORY
IMMEDIATE
MARRIAGE
MOTHER

ONCE-REMOVED
PARENT
PHOTOGRAPH
RECORD
RELATIVE
RESEARCH
SISTER
UNCLE
YOUNGER

# 121 THINGS THAT ARE HEAVY

```
H U T F A R C R I A K L R A C
A E D K C O R E L E P H A N T
E I T L K I T S O F A D A R P
O E A C O E R N R A N E A V D
H R I N A G K P M C R I K S A
O R B E O U F R I O N H E A E
B B S P N I A H C A A R E N I
E O T I O H S R E M K T O C F
O O A A G I B I M E E C O H P
C K T N R P F E V O R L U O W
W C U O E P R R D E D T A R F
F A E H B O N R I P L V N H T
E S I O E E T E I D L E T N W
N E B G C C G H H E G C T R C
C O I H I G S C A C N E T E L
```

AIRCRAFT
ANCHOR
BOOKCASE
BRICK
CHAIN
ELEPHANT
FRIDGE
GOLD
HAMMER
HIPPO
ICEBERG

PIANO
ROCK
SHIP
SOFA
STATUE
TELEVISION
TREE
TRUCK
WHALE

# TIME FOR A TEST 122

```
I D T L S I P R A C T I C E I
Q U E S T I O N S S S C S R A
M U L T I P L E C H O I C E C
N T M T S E T S S L L S T S O
I O E E D A R G T E R Y K U N
N S T U D Y E Y N E A N Z L C
G N I K R A M C W S O E E T E
I R E M N N E S S W A S D O N
C R E C R P N E L M D E E N T
D U R R O A N E C S E L R E R
I N D I G N D Z I P I I E O A
A R N C D G N T S I C C S U T
E T I A E E N I L N O N A A I
S T P R E P A R E D S E R T O
C S P R E M I T T S D P E S N
```

ANSWERS
CONCENTRATION
ERASER
ESSAY
GRADE
KNOWLEDGE
MARKING
MULTIPLE
CHOICE
ONLINE
PENCIL

POINTS
PRACTICE
PREPARE
QUESTIONS
RESULT
SILENCE
SPEED
STUDY
TEST
TIMER

# FOUR-LETTER NAMES: BOYS

**123**

```
A A N G S O C D L A N T I M A
L E A A Z S R R N O M Z L L S
G U O D W R O S W H L O E C N
C N J R O A Y E L A E X S T T
A E E R C L N R B N B D E E A
R R O U A T W E O K A A M L A
R T Z E A N O L E R R H A D D
R X O E D A L E L C T Y T A N
O E C H U G O A N W G J T K L
N E E E D H L S A W W C O O T
N D O L J A I L J E N S D E Z
U L W E O T T J J R A D J O L
L O Y X O C C A J D A O I N A
N A C N N H H C A S G A E L H
N R L O D A H K H L L C L S A
```

| | |
|---|---|
| ABEL | HANK |
| ALEX | HUGO |
| AMOS | JACK |
| COLE | JOEL |
| DALE | LARS |
| DASH | MATT |
| DOUG | OTIS |
| DREW | OWEN |
| ELON | RORY |
| EZRA | WALT |

# FOUR-LETTER NAMES: GIRLS

124

```
A E A R R I A I N E O A A S I
E L I E O A A A A D I A E R A
A T Z T R O A H J K R T A A S
L I A O N H S U A E N R N D E
A S N A U A N I R L A I C J A
A L A N H E A R A R N A O Z I
L A E A A T A L Y H A A R R Y
S A L R C H U A N L A A A S M
R E L A A E A R L A L A E A R
O L A R R B Y U I M S E T R N
S N I E Y E A E A R O A N A S
C L T L T A E I L I E S L R J
N A R O A T H E R E L O P A E
E A L N O A A R H E C A R A Z
I K R E Y A A A A T K E E A A
```

| | |
|---|---|
| AINE | ISLA |
| ARYA | JUNE |
| ASHA | KAIA |
| CARY | LILA |
| CLEO | NELL |
| CORA | NINA |
| ELLA | NORA |
| ETTA | RUTH |
| HEBE | SARA |
| IRMA | ZARA |

# 125 MAKING A SALAD

```
D G T M A I A A E T A M E C L
D N O I D S S W C E L E V I P
I I E X D I E A U N R D V R E
E S L T V P V S T A I A P A E
T S I O I T A H T D T U N C L
A E O G N E E C E D T C R S V
L R D E E V L E L I L O P A E
P D D T G E E S N P U H U S G
A D A H A A V A U T D A P E E
N D L E R B B E O E E L O O T
O A E R O O C N U S B A H T A
T S E S W I S H V I E R C A B
U V L L L S B R E H A U D M L
P E T S D H E A D U E A T O E
E R E N N I P S D A L A S T S
```

ADD DRESSING
ADD OIL
ADD VINEGAR
CHOP UP
CROUTONS
HERBS
LEAVES
LETTUCE
MIX TOGETHER
PEEL

VEGETABLES
PUT IN A BOWL
PUT ON A PLATE
SALAD SPINNER
SLICE UP
TOMATOES
WASH

```
R M C R T B U T T O N K Y U M
T I N K C A N H F A C U F F T
E K C A B T P H C A N O R I S
U M M O E E C E E T B R C D E
N R A D L T E S M E A R O O V
T B E C I L O C O E M P I E E
T T Z T H K A R N A A R E C E
E E S U M I C R E L N S R T L
K T D T N L N S R R N D U C S
C N T L E R L E E R F A L R D
O T L V A I V T I E B E E R E
P E R A F Z T B I U E R R C N
B O E C C A B E Y E I H O U A
P A S A P O R D O R V T M T O
P S L T N N E L D E E N E T I
```

| | |
|---|---|
| BUTTON | PATTERN |
| COLLAR | POCKET |
| CUFF | RIBBON |
| CUT | RULER |
| FABRIC | SEAM |
| IRON | SLEEVE |
| KNIT | STITCH |
| MACHINE | TAPE MEASURE |
| NEEDLE | THREAD |
| PATCH | VELCRO |

# THINGS YOU CAN READ

**127**

```
D P                             S I
R U Y                       T N E
A Z R E                 O S N M
C Z A W M           R T C O A
T L N L A E       Y R Y R W G
S E O I N E O T T U C G E R A
O B I A U A S P C L U I C O Z
P O T M A I I T O I V U I D I
N O C E L E I P D E C D P R N
N K I N C O E E R E T T E L E
  T D E N D L A R T I C L E
    R S I N G I S D A O R
      A R R T P I R C S
        Y A L E V O N
          E M T
```

ARTICLE
DICTIONARY
EMAIL
ENCYCLOPEDIA
GUIDE
INSTRUCTIONS
LETTER
LIST
MAGAZINE
MANUAL
NOVEL
POEM

POSTCARD
PUZZLE BOOK
RECEIPT
RECIPE
REVIEW
ROAD SIGN
SCRIPT
STORY

# ISLAND COUNTRIES 128

```
A A S O U A N G R E N A D A A
J E D U C A C I T A A S B U S
J D O N U Y S I A N I A M N U
A U A R A F P J A N O A A E V
P S U N N L G R G M A A D I A
A D A D A A A A U T A E A N N
N O K I A U P E U S N J G D U
A M N E C O S V Z S D S A O A
I I A W R U A T B W A S S N T
C N L E A L L A R U E A C E U
E I I I U M H T R A L N A S N
L C R R O R E N N S L A R I I
A A S N A W I A T I A I N A A
N I K I R I B A T I A E A E A
D M N U B A R B A D O S N A B
```

| | |
|---|---|
| AUSTRALIA | NAURU |
| BAHRAIN | NEW ZEALAND |
| BARBADOS | SAINT LUCIA |
| CYPRUS | SINGAPORE |
| DOMINICA | SRI LANKA |
| GRENADA | TAIWAN |
| ICELAND | TUVALU |
| INDONESIA | VANUATU |
| JAMAICA | |
| JAPAN | |
| KIRIBATI | |
| MADAGASCAR | |

# TRICKY SPELLINGS

129

```
M R A C S I W L T C A S T H Y
U T N S A P A E E H A S H R E
G H A G T L E Y A N G U Y U H
N O T A Y R E C R A O I G C I
E U D T G A A N I A S L E H I
G G E D T B D I D A U T O W T
R H A N N P R S G A L R H C L
B T A U O A I E E H R L B M F
I A O L G U L E A N T N E E A
U R E I T N G S C T D G A R F
Q U E U E A A H I E H E E H U
T H R O U G H L I E R E W I L
A L T E S S A R R A B M E U M
U F S T O E S I R P R U S T W
A N A U G H T Y R S D S H E E
```

ASTHMA
BREATHE
CALENDAR
CAUGHT
COLONEL
EMBARRASS
ENOUGH
FEBRUARY
ISLAND
LANGUAGE
NAUGHTY

QUEUE
RECEIPT
SPECIAL
STRAIGHT
SURPRISE
THOUGHT
THROUGH
WEDNESDAY
WEIGHT

# WORDS FROM SHAKESPEARE

```
D I B E M A J E S T I C E T E
Y E A A R A Y W B B S X I J A
S L W T T U L G Z A C B I I Q
E O I A E B S D W I N D L E M
R C I U L K A O T M O D E U E
N N N W Q F N E P A L G I L X
O H B A C N M A M X A E B T G
I P O E I E A A L G E A E E E
P E L B N D Z R G B N R N B L
M D H T N E A U T O U E E O F
A A H A M O L R I T R D N U F
H N D E E F B H X O R S L A U
C T N N G D S I U O B P A N C
B T C I R A F S O B D A E I S
A N L N F O N M L L A B E Y E
```

| | |
|---|---|
| AMAZEMENT | FIXTURE |
| BANDIT | FLAWED |
| BEDROOM | GENEROUS |
| BLANKET | HOBNOB |
| CHAMPION | LUGGAGE |
| DWINDLE | MAJESTIC |
| EXCITEMENT | PEDANT |
| EXPOSURE | RADIANCE |
| EYEBALL | SCUFFLE |
| FASHIONABLE | TRANQUIL |

# 131

# IT CONTAINS FIVE "I"S

```
I N D I V I D U A L I S T I C
R N I N E L I G I B I L I T Y
R Y S N I I T N I B N T T A T
E I I E V I E N I D I I G I
S S N L N I I G V L I I T R I
I T T V L S G T I I V E G Y I
S I I T I I I L N V I E S I N
T N L I I S B T C T S L N Y I
I M P O S S I B I L I T I E S
B L G T I L L B B V B I Y Z S
I I N I T I A L I Z I N G T I
L Y C I L S L I L L L T I I N
I N T E L L I G I B I L I T Y
T L Y C I R B I T N T T I E I
Y E E S I I T N Y I Y D Y I S
```

IMPOSSIBILITIES
INDIVIDUALISTIC
INDIVISIBILITY
INELIGIBILITY
INITIALIZING
INSENSITIVITIES
INTELLIGIBILITY
INVINCIBILITY

INVISIBILITY
IRRESISTIBILITY

# GET STARTED

**1**
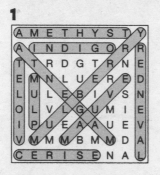

**2**

**3**

**4**
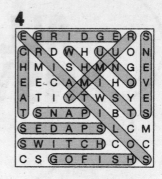

**5**

**6**
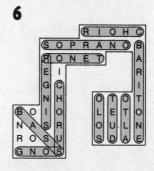

**7**

**8**

**9**

**10**

**11**

**12**

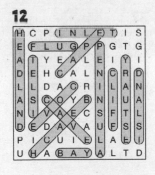

**13**

```
W O Y R R U L F U E
H G T N E R R U C R
I L B R E E Z E R R
R W F L R H T B H C
L O L S G W R S Y B
F H P U F F O C U R
H T A E R B L L N G
Y E L A G O L Y B W
T F A W N R W U U W
N E W E W H O O S H
```

**14**

```
O A V E N U E L S V
O E K P A T H S T L
W G C W H A A E R K
T R A I L P E Y P W
S L R C R R E A O A
A L T E T L S W S L
L E D S L S W H S K
W N W A A A L G A A
U A Y G R W E I A Y
K L E R O A D H G Y
```

**15**

```
I A I L O G N O M D
C A E N A E Z R A N
E D I S O T T I W A
L A L S T R V C A L
A N D I S O W I K N
N A O K O U N A A I
D C H I N A R I Y F
K A Z A K H S T A N
S W E D E N M A R K
N A T S Z Y G R Y K
```

**16**

```
Y T S I L K C E H C
Y R O T N E V N I O
S R A R E T S O R N
Y A E L A R O T A T
L D X G U G R E U E
L N Y E I B E C D N
A E A B D S A N E T
B L E B S N T C D S
U A S M E T I E O A
S C H E D U L E R V
```

**17**

```
M O O R H S U M O L
E A O D A C O V A N A C
O S O E P U H C T E K C
  I H F E N E O P
B L A I R N U A A U
H A E N T I N A L G
I S C T N O E H A
S T I O T O M D J A
  M O L N U Y A E
A E S E E H C A T G L
S M U S T A R D E M O G
R O N O I N O D E I R P
```

**18**

```
S N M D E E W A E S
P T I S E L I A N S
O M U H I U E B T P
N L U M C N R A C M
G E P S O R R R I R
E E L M S F U N A H
T E E K I E R A B
K N K S N C L C E S
A E H E B I K L S S
S W H E L K W E N H
```

**19**

**20**

**21**

**22**

**23**

**24**

**25**

```
F R R N L U N H T R R
I N T T R I R R O N E
S K M L I E E L I I
I R N S F K L A T T I
L O N T R E T L F L L
T F O A R N L R O E
L I M B U T E T A A N
E L A O S U L Y T S I
G L F E I L T O L I F
L T N I O P L L A B P
H I G H L I G H T E R
```

**26**

```
F N R E R R I T S C M
I S M R R R L H R I L
L T A A K M S E R P E
E T U R E D A D L O M
R U P L O B C N S M A
A A P C P O R C A E M
E P C P D O R L T P I
E E E P E I P F E S H
R T R C S S R R R R H
```

**27**

```
L G O E B S W N G N N
U U S K P V E S O A O
H W G E N G I N E O I
V B S G K T A I G E S
E A A E E A N A G C E
N C E H S G B E C K E
T S E D L E G S A P
S T H G I L E R N R S
B E I S A A G E A B U
A W O D N I W E H C S
W I I N A K S G T W K
```

**28**

```
L I N G U I N E I I E
I E N T O T N N L L I
T L R I L I L N L O N
E A I U P L T P C V I
H F T S P A E I I A A
G R T I I I L T M R G
A A N L C E L N R O I
P F G L T G V M E O R
S A R U E N N I V S T
T I N O L L E N N A C
```

**29**

```
G E N F L M N X G I Y
C X O A A T R O T N E
M P I N E A A O O A R
A E T A T D L I W I R
E C A L N S N I S I P
D A I I Y B H N G O R
Y A I T G M P P N T H
A I D O M A E R I S E D
R N U I T L A T N G A R
```

**30**

```
E E N A P O R P Y T C
I B I O M A S S T D O
N T U R B I N E E A A
T A W A V E S H C D L
O I G W I N D Y E I S
I S C E M L D N N R E
S I R A O L T R E U L
I O O H I L R C S O C
F N G T S S A G E T I
R E E U I H O G L U M
N M F R A L O S E M N
```

**31**

```
W K E L B B I R C S P
N E S E T D P E O O D
S S T J L O E O D E S
H A T W T E T O X I I U
D R R A L U G O T C E
E A I I R N O Y D D T
Y C N W T C I H P N C
U E K R A M S M L O H
P I C T U R E S S I C
I L L U S T R A T E S
```

**32**

```
A N E T        A T T E N D C
N A T E        S T A N N O S
T E T N        I N T E N N I
E N I          X E N I T T A S
N I A          E N N T O F T E
I N T E        T I E T F T N E
N T E          N I T D N T E
T E N          I O C O D N N C
E I D          C O B O N N A E
N C I          U T E N S I L
S E            N E T S I L N
```

**33**

```
L S L M E C I L S W S
P O L I S H E E O L D
L M U D W H L N I E F
A M E A S D S M E S E
L E I U D E E P R E X
H C L U M F A E D H A
G S P L S N B S L S W
L L N W A P S G O R F
L A I N S I E F I S H
U E A O E S O A P A C
D B G R E A S E P A I
```

**34**

```
E N O T S D E T E D K
W L T S L A T E C D C
W O E C U T L E R Y I
L A O E W H A M M E R
L D L D T E M L E H B
E N A L U S C N L T L
H O E L B B E P N O E
S M E R O C K E C I D
E A A C O N C R E T E
R I T E L B R A M C T
L D E H D E A E U C R
```

**35**

```
R B B L A Z E R A I Z
E L R S S L T A E H R
S H I R T C S S E T O
E N H B S W E O Z B T
R R A S E S R C C S K
S I A A K S R C C S K
O S T C T T B S B A T
B E O T E R E E A R I
R S M R M I G O R T E
I Z K E A K A H A T A
S A T G N S B B S S K E
```

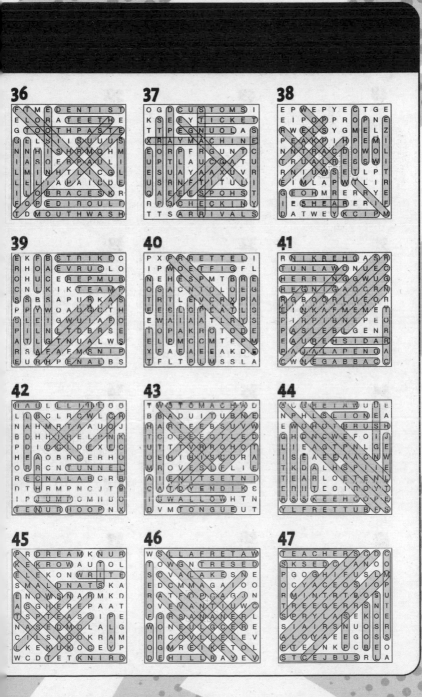

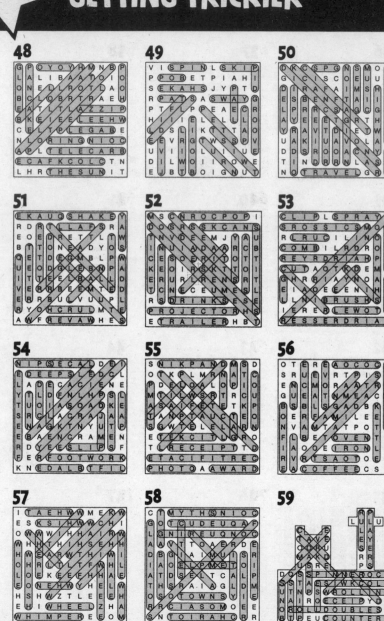

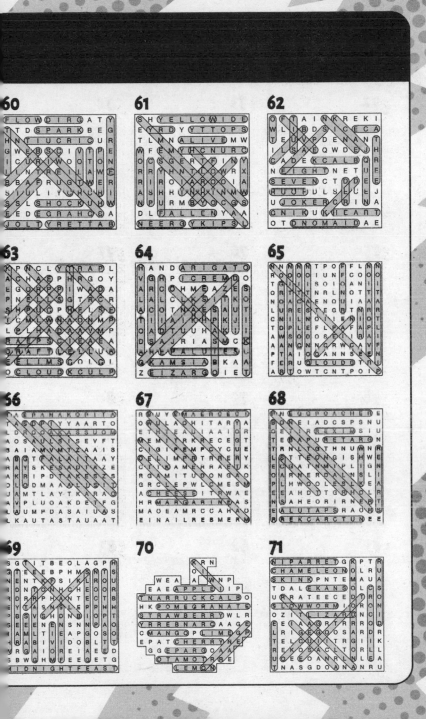

# GETTING TRICKIER

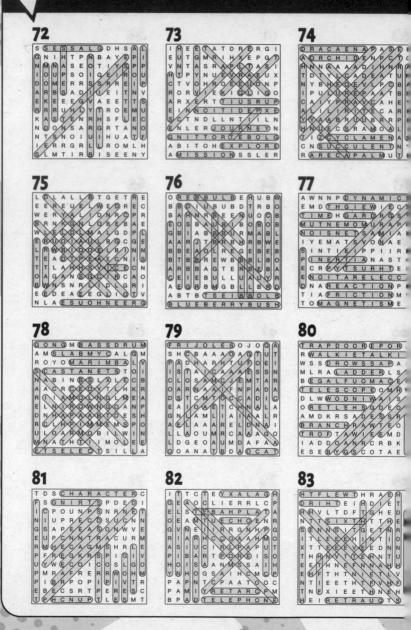

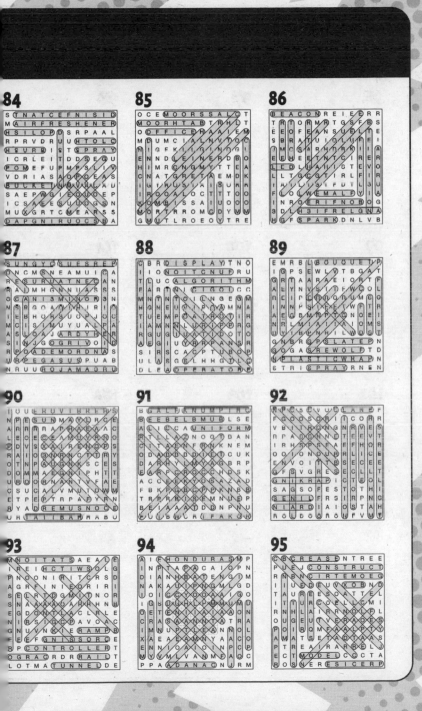

# GETTING TRICKIER

## 96

## 97

## 98

## 99

## 100

## 101

## 102

## 103
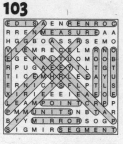

## 104

# EXPERTS ONLY

## 105

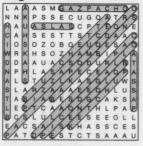

## 106

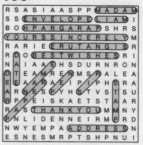

## 107

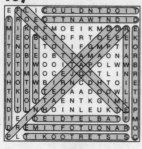

## 108

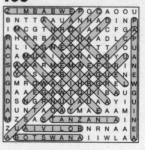

## 109

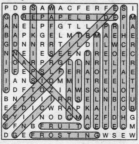

## 110

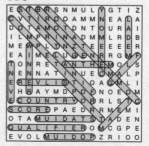

**111**

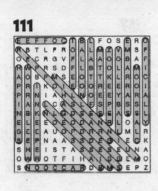

**112**

**113**

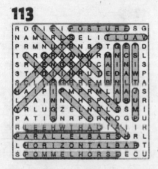

**114**

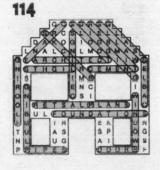

**115**

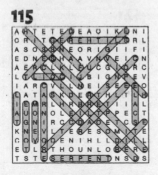

# EXPERTS ONLY

## 116

## 117

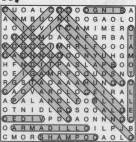

## 118

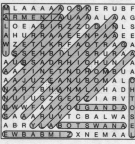

## 119

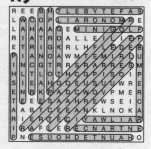

## 120

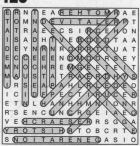

## 121

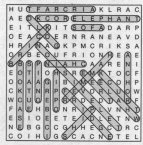

## 122

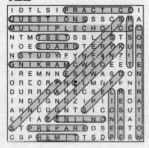

## 123

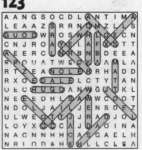

## 124

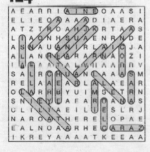

## 125

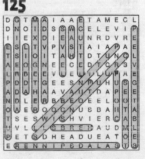

## 126

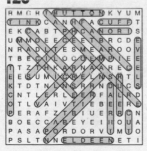

## 127

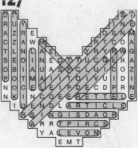

**128**

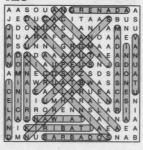

**129**

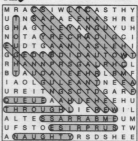

**130**

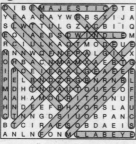

**131**

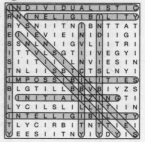

First published in Great Britain in 2023 by Buster Books,
an imprint of Michael O'Mara Books Limited,
9 Lion Yard, Tremadoc Road, London SW4 7NQ

 www.mombooks.com/buster

 Buster Books

 @BusterBooks

@buster_books

Puzzles and solutions © Gareth Moore 2023
Illustrations and layouts © Buster Books 2023
Images adapted from www.shutterstock.com

A CIP catalogue record for this book is available from the British Library.

ISBN: 978-1-78055-972-8

1  3  5  7  9  10  8  6  4  2

This product is made of material from well-managed, FSC®-certified
forests and other controlled sources. The manufacturing processes
conform to the environmental regulations of the country of origin.

This book was printed in July 2023 by
CPI Group (UK) Ltd, Croydon, CR0 4YY.

MIX
Paper | Supporting
responsible forestry
FSC® C171272